SPICE BOX

Grace Regan

EBURY
PRESS

*To Auntie Dolly for inspiring
a dream, to Mum and Dad
for helping to make it happen.*

SPiCEBOX

CONTENTS

iNTRODUCTiON

I'd like to begin this book by addressing an important issue up front. As a white British woman who cooks curry for a living, I am well aware that I tread sensitive ground. It is crucial for me to acknowledge that there is a fine line between paying respect to the culinary history of India and cultural appropriation. As you read on, I hope it becomes clear that everything I do comes from a place of deep love and respect for India. I will never profess to be an 'expert' on the incredibly rich, diverse and complex cuisine of India; I prefer to think of myself as an enthusiastic student. The recipes in this book are not 'authentic' – they draw inspiration from the incredible British-Indian curry houses I grew up eating in, as well as the home cooking I have been fortunate enough to eat when visiting my Auntie Dolly's house and India. I owe everything I know to the true masters of this topic – Indian home cooks, who have been so generous in taking the time to teach me their craft and share their knowledge with me.

. . . .

India has always played a significant role in my life. This is mainly thanks to my great aunt Dolly, who is from Chennai (formerly known as Madras) in South India. At 90, Dolly is still as much the charismatic force to be reckoned with as she was when I was a young child. She is a huge inspiration to me, full of wisdom, humour and, of course, culinary prowess (although she'd never admit to the latter).

Auntie Dolly married my mother's uncle Pea and, as a result, Mum has spent a lot of time travelling around India. Her own mother is buried in Delhi – she died during a trip visiting her brother in the city. Growing up, I'd listen to Mum waxing lyrical about the country she loved so much, counting down the years until I too could visit.

Before I had the chance to visit India myself, I was exposed to the wonders of its cuisine once Auntie Dolly and Uncle Pea had moved back to the UK. I will never forget the cloud of aromas that engulfed me as soon as I walked through the door of their house – a pot of simmering dhal wafting notes of turmeric, a pan of buttery pilau rice fragrant with saffron and a plate of samosas already laid out on the table for us to snack on.

I was 18 the first time I went to India and, as soon as I stepped off the plane, I knew I'd inherited my mother's love of the country – since then, I've returned every year. Over the years, as my interest in cooking grew, so did my ambition to learn from any home cook who'd have me. Many of my holidays in India were – and still are! – spent standing next to the gas stove of a generous host, scribbling down notes as I watched them throw spices into bubbling oil, trying to convert pinches and handfuls into teaspoons and grams. Great home cooks

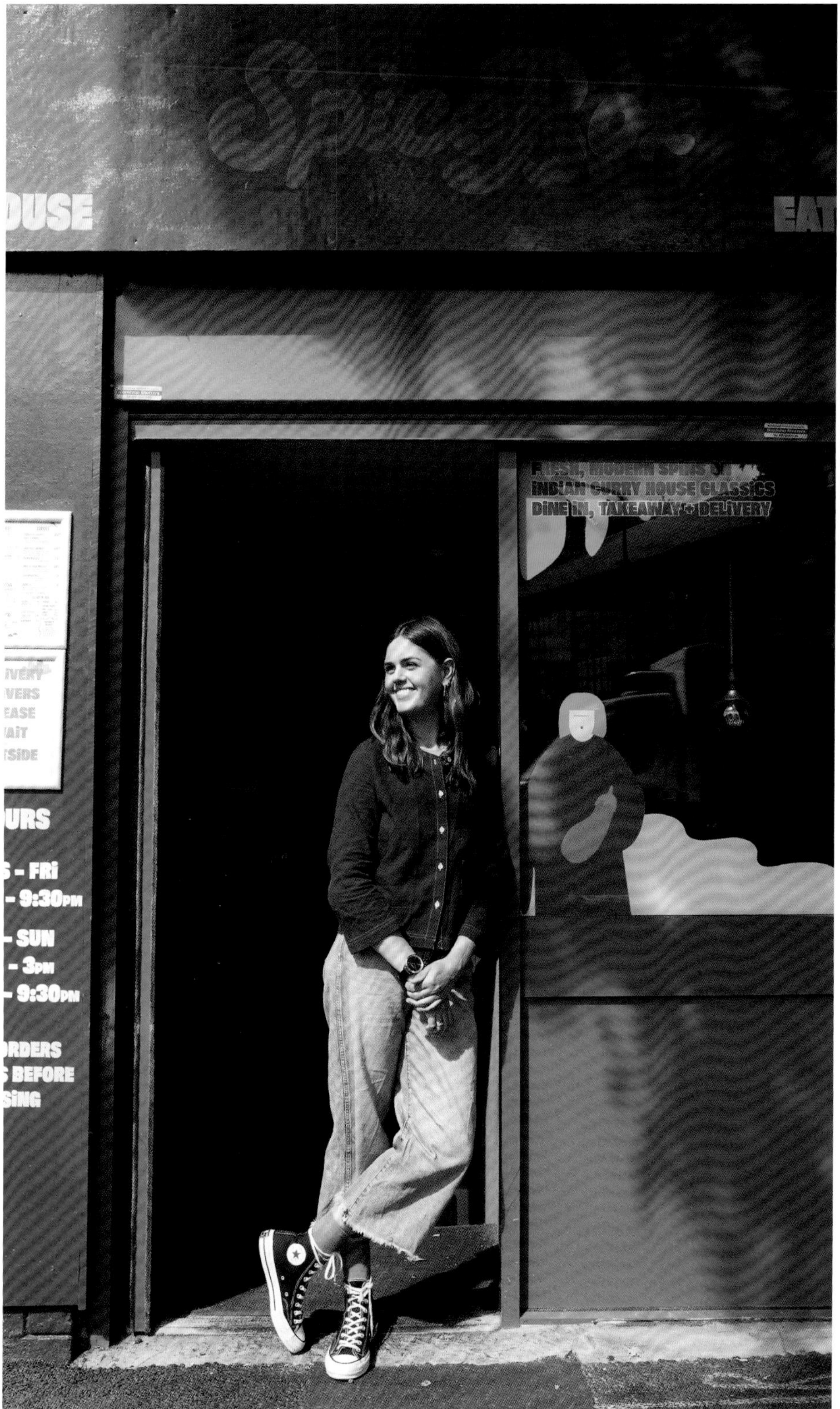
INDIAN CURRY HOUSE CLASSICS
DINE IN, TAKEAWAY + DELIVERY

never write down recipes. Over the past few years, I've also tried to coax recipes out of Dolly (who, again, writes nothing down), some of which you'll find in this book.

It is therefore no surprise that I have ended up cooking curry for a living.

I first came up with the idea for SpiceBox around six years ago while on a trip to South India with Mum. I was thinking about my imminent return to London and how much I'd miss eating dhals, dosas and thorans every day. I wondered why – even though there were loads of incredible Indian takeaways and curry houses near me in East London – I struggled to find the sort of fresh, veg-led food I had been eating in India, without making an excursion to Wembley or Southall. I thought how amazing it would be to find a local curry house in London serving food that tasted like the dishes home cooks such as Auntie Dolly made.

Don't get me wrong, I LOVE eating at British-Indian curry houses – when you're in the mood, nothing hits the spot like a deep pink tikka masala, a sweet and sour dhansak or a fried ball of onion bhaji – after all these are all versions of Indian dishes that were adapted to suit a Western palate. But, I thought, wouldn't it be cool to merge the best of British Indian food with the fresher flavours of Indian home cooking – and so the idea for SpiceBox was born.

My curry-house dreams were put on hold as soon as I returned to the UK. I was building a tech start-up at the time and, shortly after my holiday, found out that I had been accepted onto an accelerator programme in Silicon Valley. This was too good an opportunity to turn down and so I packed my bags and moved to California.

In California I became vegan. I had been vegetarian for years and had tried to go vegan a number of times but I'd always found it so difficult – and quite frankly depressing – in London. But in California, in the summer of 2015, there was no excuse. The vegan food scene was exploding, and on weekends I would travel with my business partner Sagar to Berkley, Oakland, LA and, of course, San Francisco to seek out every cool new vegan restaurant or street food truck. The more vegan food I ate, and the more reading I did around veganism, the more invested in it I became. To me, it was such an easy, enjoyable way to do my bit for the planet and my health.

As my interest in vegan food was growing, my engagement with the tech world, my business and Silicon Valley was dwindling. I had fallen out of love with what I was doing and it was slowly eating away at my soul. After a lot of sleepless nights and mini breakdowns, I finally decided to pull the plug on what I was working on. The question of what to do next was a no-brainer.

The idea of SpiceBox was still swimming around in the back of my mind, and I began to draw connections between this and my new-found love of vegetables. Indian food was the perfect way to introduce people to a plant-based diet – after all, various religious and cultural groups have been eating vegan dishes for

thousands of years in India. Even the most ardent meat-eaters are familiar with the concept of a vegetarian curry, and spices are the best way to add complexity and flavour to vegetables.

And so, I moved back to London to put this curry-house dream into action. Within a week of returning to the UK, I started developing the SpiceBox menu from my home kitchen. I'd cook by day and cycle containers of warm curry to friends' houses by night, for them to try and give feedback on. Once I had landed on a menu, I got a small table built to fit in my doorway and turned my home into an Indian takeaway. For two months, I stayed home six nights a week, waiting by the phone for an order. I was lucky if I got five orders a night. But slowly, word of mouth began to spread. To my relief, people liked my cooking and started to tell their friends about SpiceBox. Before long, the *Evening Standard* had caught wind and featured one of my curries in their list of London's best vegetarian dishes.

I was now ready to take the next step and, after lots of emails and taste tests, landed a stall at Druid Street market in Bermondsey. Here I met a lovely trader called Tom who introduced me to Kerb, a street food collective that runs markets across London. They were looking for a new vegan trader.

And so began two and a half years of being a street food trader, trading at markets and festivals up and down the country. I had never worked as hard as I did then – and probably never will again. Going from cooking curry in my home kitchen to feeding thousands at music festivals was a serious baptism of fire but it taught me quickly how to run a food business and cook at scale. I went from not knowing how to put up a small tent, to erecting a 3-metre-square gazebo and building a temporary kitchen every day, only to pack it down again two hours later once lunch service was over. I became the proud owner of a VW Transporter van and a dab hand with cable ties; I learnt how to replace blown fuses, build signage and cook 600 portions of dhal at 5am in an electric pan (we ran out of food at the first festival we did!).

After over two years of life on the road, I was ready to lay some roots for SpiceBox. I raised investment and, in a twist of fate and good luck, met Alpesh who had far more experience running restaurants than I did. I convinced him to come on board and started looking for our first curry house. I eventually found the perfect space on Hoe Street in Walthamstow and in January 2019 we opened our doors.

Since opening, we've been full almost every night, won multiple awards and built up the most amazing loyal following of local guests, who come back week after week to feast on our fresh spins on curry-house classics. Our food has stayed true to my original concept – SpiceBox pays homage to British Indian curry-house cuisine and traditional Indian home cooking in equal measure.

I am hugely passionate about the joys of eating more vegetables, and with this book I hope to teach you how to use spices and Indian-inspired cooking methods to get the best out of plant-based food. In 2021, it sounds a bit passé to wang on

about how destructive industrial animal agriculture is for the environment, but we need to keep talking about it until the problem is solved. I'm not here to try to turn anyone vegan, but I am here to hopefully show you how delicious, satisfying and complex vegan food can be. With this, I hope you may be tempted to eat at least one vegan meal a week.

I also hope to teach you a little about Indian cooking. As I addressed at the start, I am aware that I must tread this ground delicately and accept the fact that I am a student of Indian food as opposed to an expert. I do believe that everyone has the ability to become a great curry-cooker. At its heart, cooking is really just an equation – with the same key principles for each dish – and it is my aim that, once you've cooked a handful of recipes from this book, you'll be able to start to decode the fundamental formula of Indian cooking. The build-your-own charts in the book are designed to help you get to grips with this, but all it really comes down to is practice. Soon enough, you'll start to get creative with your curries and, using this book as a reference point, you'll be able to rustle up something delicious from whatever you have lying around in your fridge and cupboards.

Stay spicy!
Grace

HOW TO GET THE BEST OUT OF VEG

I LOVE vegetables. I'm evangelical about them. I've devoted my career to them. And I want you to love them as much as I do.

This will be easy – you just have to learn how to prepare and cook them the right way. Without the right amount of seasoning, or suitable cooking method, vegetables can be bland, soggy affairs. Yes, seasonality and quality do come into play but, if you follow the pointers laid out below, you'll be able to transform even the palest, saddest supermarket veg into something splendid.

AUBERGINE

Preparing

People used to salt aubergines to help remove their bitterness. Modern varieties are sweeter and so some say there's no longer any need to salt them. I don't agree. Cutting aubergines into chunks, sprinkling with salt and leaving them to rest for 10 minutes before cooking helps to slacken their taut flesh by removing water. This helps them become even better flavour sponges. I always use fine sea salt when salting aubergines as it is easier to distribute evenly. I don't bother rinsing my aubergines after salting them, I just slightly reduce the amount of salt I add during cooking. After all, salt and aubergines are a great combo!

Cooking

Smoking: If you're making the Smoky Aubergine and Pea Curry on pages 60–2, the best way to cook your aubergine is by smoking it over a flame. This is only possible if you have a gas hob or BBQ. For gas, pierce the aubergine all over with a fork and use tongs to sit it on top of a high flame from a medium ring. Leave for 5 minutes until the skin is completely charred, then turn it over so you can char the other side. Repeat until it is charred all the way around, and the skin is almost falling away from the soft middle. Place it in a colander over a bowl to cool down. When the aubergine is cool enough to handle, peel away the black skin with your hands and discard. I often save the smoky dark juice to add back into the dish I'm cooking for extra flavour.

If you're smoking your aubergine on a BBQ and you've got a good flame going, use the same method as above. If not, place the whole aubergine directly on the glowing embers, rotating every 5 minutes until cooked.

Roasting: Cut your aubergines into 2.5cm chunks, sprinkle them with salt and leave for 10 minutes. Drizzle evenly with a generous amount of veg oil and roast in an oven set to 180°C for 30–40 minutes until they're soft and caramelised.

Frying: Prepare the aubergine as above. The secret to frying aubergine well is patience. You need to start by heating a generous amount of veg oil (around 6 tablespoons) in a pan on a medium heat. As soon as you add the aubergine, it will soak up every millilitre of that oil but, after 5 minutes of frying, the skin will begin to slacken, releasing the oil back into the pan. From this point, a bit more cooking turns the flesh buttery and soft and the skin gloriously crispy – around 10–15 minutes should do it.

BROCCOLI

Preparing

Most recipes will call for florets of broccoli. I find the easiest way to get florets is by using my hands to break the mini broccoli trees from the main trunk (or stalk). I hate throwing away broccoli stalks. All you need to do is slice it nice and thin and cook it with your florets – it is perfectly edible and adds a nice contrast in texture.

Some recipes (e.g. Curry-crusted Tandoori Broccoli on page 88) ask for 'steaks' – this can be achieved by simply slicing the broccoli head in half lengthways down the middle.

Long, thin florets, such as sprouting or Tenderstem broccoli, work best for stir-frying or sautéing, as they cook quicker. When adding broccoli to a curry, I often choose this kind as I can chuck it straight into the sauce and cook it in 5 minutes.

Cooking

Boiling and blanching : Forget the soggy, bland boiled broccoli of your school days, broccoli cooked this way can taste amazing, as long as you season your water properly. Fill a medium saucepan with water and add 2 tablespoons of fine sea salt – it should taste as salty as the sea. Bring it to a rapid boil and add the broccoli. Boil for 5 minutes or until your broccoli is cooked how you like it – sometimes I'm in the mood for super-soft and other times nice and crunchy. Drain in a colander and leave to steam-dry for a few minutes. I always add a squeeze of lemon and pinch of pepper to boiled broccoli before I eat it.

Blanching should be done in exactly the same way – just take the broccoli out after a minute or so, when it's turned a dark shade of green.

Roasting: When roasting broccoli steaks, I usually blanch them first, otherwise I find they dy out and burn before they have cooked through.

Place your blanched broccoli in a roasting tin. Drizzle with veg oil and sprinkle with salt and pepper. Roast in an oven at 180°C for 25–35 minutes until it's crispy and charred on the outside and cooked through in the middle. Again, finish with a squeeze of lemon. If you're just roasting florets, you can skip the blanching step.

Stir-frying/sautéing: Heat a tablespoon of veg oil in a frying pan and add the broccoli. Fry for 5–10 minutes until it turns a darker shade of green and begins to char in places. Finish with a sprinkling of salt and a squeeze of lemon.

CABBAGE

I am a big fan of cabbage. I think it might be our most underrated vegetable and I've taken it upon myself to become a lobbyist for this affordable, multi-seasonal brassica. Like most veg, it's all down to the cooking, but first a quick word on varieties. You'll find many different types on supermarket shelves, all with their own merits – from the crinkle-leaved Savoy to the deep purple red cabbage. For most of the dishes in this book, I prefer the pointed sweet cabbage or classic round green cabbage.

Preparing

I prepare cabbage one of two ways – either by chopping it into thick wedges and charring it on a BBQ or smoking hot griddle (see below) or by cutting it in half and then thinly shredding it with a knife.

Cooking

Charring: Cut your cabbage into thick wedges (unless it's huge, simply quarter it from the top). Rub the wedges with veg oil and sprinkle with salt, then set to one side for 10 minutes to give the salt and oil time to soften the thicker outer leaves. Heat a cast-iron griddle or heavy-based frying pan on a high heat until it's smoking hot, or get your BBQ ready. Place the wedges flat-side down and leave for 3 minutes or until they are nicely charred and slightly softened. Turn and repeat until all sides are done. You can then shred the charred cabbage and add it to salads, sabzis or curries for a crunchy, smoky kick. Alternatively, you can eat the wedges as they are, drizzled with lemon, oil and salt.

Stir-frying/sautéing: This is how I cook the cabbage for all the recipes in this book. Fry the thinly shredded cabbage in an oiled pan until it softens. It's best to start off on a high heat so you get some browning, then turn down the heat to get it nice and soft (this

will take 15–20 minutes). Cabbage loves a good pinch of salt when it hits the pan and a squeeze of lemon once it's cooked.

CARROTS

Preparing

The only rule I have for prepping carrots is *DO NOT PEEL THEM*. Firstly, it's a waste of your precious time on planet Earth. Secondly, it's a waste of carrot. The skins are perfectly edible and nutritious. If your carrots are a little muddy or hairy, just give them a good old scrub in cold water. After that, it's up to you – dice them, slice them, baton them. For slow-cooking curries, I tend to roughly dice my carrots into 1cm chunks and cook them in the curry sauce. Alternatively, adding roasted carrots (see below) works well too. When I want a crunchier carrot, for things like a stir-fry or light summery curry, I cut the carrots diagonally into thin slices and add them towards the end of cooking.

Cooking

Boiling: Here's a tip you'll use for the rest of your life – if a vegetable grows underground, you should always place it in cold water and bring it (gradually) to the boil. If a vegetable grows above ground, you should put it straight into boiling water. You're welcome!

Put your prepped carrots in a saucepan and cover them with cold water and 2 tablespoons of fine sea salt. Bring them to the boil and simmer until they're cooked (this will take around 30 minutes). Drain and steam-dry for a few minutes to get rid of any excess water. You shouldn't need to season the carrots as they will have absorbed the salt during cooking.

Roasting: When roasting carrots, diagonally slice them into thin rounds or cut them into batons. Place them in a roasting tin, drizzle with veg oil and sprinkle with salt and a pinch of cumin seeds. Roast in an oven at 180°C until they're soft in the middle and nice and caramelised on the outside (around 30 minutes).

Stir-frying/sautéing: Cut your carrots diagonally into thin slices and throw them into a hot, oiled frying pan, adding a pinch of salt when they hit the pan. Fry until they're cooked but still have some crunch (around 10 minutes).

CAULiFLOWER

You may or may not know by now that cauliflower is my favourite vegetable. I am therefore *very* keen to make sure you cook it well! Nobody puts cauli in the corner.

Preparing

Cauliflower can be prepared a number of ways. The first rule is not to throw away all of the leaves. The outer, tougher leaves can be used to make veg stock (see page 32) and the inner leaves can be boiled or roasted with the cauliflower – they are particularly good roasted as they go super-crispy.

The most common way to prep cauliflower is to cut it into small florets – you can use your hands to break little trees off the central trunk (stalk) or use a knife. Never throw away the stalk, simply thinly slice it and cook with the florets.

I often 'steak' cauliflower. First, trim the end of the stalk so you have a flat, even base and stand the cauliflower upright on a chopping board. Using a large knife, cut the cauli into 1.5cm-thick slices. You may end up with smaller pieces on either end but that's OK.

Cauliflower is also amazing roasted whole (see page 20). To prepare, remove the tough outer leaves but keep the inner leaves intact. If there is excess stalk, trim it with a knife so it is even and flat and your cauliflower can stand upright.

Cooking

Boiling: Cut your cauliflower into florets and place them in a saucepan of boiling water. Add 2 tablespoons of fine sea salt (it should taste as salty as the sea) and boil until the florets are nice and soft (around 15–20 minutes). I think it's best to verge on overcooking cauliflower when boiling it. If the water is perfectly salted, the cauliflower goes super-creamy and is seasoned all the way through.

Roasting: Cut the cauliflower into florets or steaks (see above), drizzle generously with veg oil and sprinkle with salt. I often sprinkle my cauli with curry powder before roasting as I think the flavours work perfectly together. Roast in an oven set to 200°C for 25–35 minutes until charred and crispy on the outside and cooked through in the middle.

Roasting whole: Prepare the cauliflower as instructed on page 18 and stand it on its stalk in an ovenproof casserole dish with a lid. Drizzle generously with veg oil, sprinkle with salt and roast in an oven set at 180°C for 1 hour. It's ready when it is soft all the way through and has turned golden on the outside. You can sub out the Curry-Crusted Tandoori Broccoli (page 88) for cauliflower cooked this way.

Grilling: Cut the cauliflower into steaks (see page 18). Drizzle with veg oil and sprinkle with salt, then set them aside for 10 minutes to allow the salt and oil to soften the steaks slightly. Heat a heavy-based frying pan or griddle pan until it's smoking hot, then add the steaks. Cook for 5 minutes on each side until golden and soft . You can also use a BBQ to cook your steaks this way. Cauli steaks are AMAZING cooked over coal – eat them slathered with the Coriander Chutney on page 213.

CUCUMBERS

Preparing

Unless I'm making a quick pickle, I don't tend to peel my cucumbers. I do, however, always deseed them. Slice them lengthways down the middle and run a teaspoon down the seedy centre – just like that, the seeds will come out. This will not only put an end to soggy cucumber salads but is also immensely satisfying.

FENNEL

Fennel has the most amazing flavour and can be added to dishes in the same way that you'd use a spice or herb to add an extra dimension.

Preparing

I usually go for thin slices of fennel. Lay the bulb flat on a chopping board and cut it lengthways into two fat halves. Then place the flat surface on a board and slice into half-moons with a sharp knife. If you're brave, you can use a mandolin (I'm not to be trusted with one). I see no need to discard any part of the fennel - slice the white flesh and green stalks. *Never* throw away the feathery fronds – they can be used as a herb to garnish fennel-based dishes or salads.

When roasting or grilling fennel, cut the bulb into thinner halves. Balance it on its side and slice lengthways down the middle. Trim off the fronds and save them to garnish.

Cooking

Stir-frying/sautéing: Thinly slice the fennel as above and fry it in a lightly oiled, hot frying pan with a pinch of salt. Cook for 10–15 minutes until the fennel has softened and turned golden in places.

Roasting: Place the fennel halves (see above), flat-side down in a roasting tin, drizzle with veg oil and sprinkle with a pinch of salt. Roast in an oven set to 180°C for 45–50 minutes until they're super-soft all the way through and almost falling apart.

Grilling: Drizzle your fennel halves with veg oil and sprinkle with salt, then leave to sit for 10 minutes. Heat a heavy-based frying pan or griddle pan until it's smoking hot, then add the fennel flat-side down. Grill until charred and soft on one side, then flip over and repeat (around 7 minutes on each side).

GARLIC

Preparing

It's fair to say that I've spent a considerable portion of my 29 years on earth prepping garlic. Peeling and chopping garlic used to be the bane of my life (a curry for 2,000 festival-goers needs *a lot* of garlic), until I discovered a few handy tricks. To quickly peel a few cloves, place them on a chopping board and use the flat side of your knife to give them a firm bash. Then slice off the woody end and the skin should come off easily. If you need to peel a lot of garlic (e.g. for the Garlic Pickle on page 227), place the cloves in a large jar or cocktail shaker and secure the lid. Shake them firmly for 30 seconds and, just like magic, the skins will come off.

Once you're past the peeling stage, things get controversial. I am a big fan of grating garlic but, over the course of sending these recipes to testers, I've learnt that some are passionately opposed to this. I believe this comes down to the grater. If you own a microplane, then I still think grating is the quickest way to get the most flavour out of your cloves. If you don't own a microplane (you have no idea what you're missing out on), then crushing them with a garlic crusher comes a close second. If you're a minimalist, with no time or budget for kitchen gadgets, thinly slicing is totally acceptable – I just recommend giving the chopped garlic a good smush with the side of your knife at the end to help release all the garlicky flavour.

Cooking

Frying: Just like you do with onions, you need to cook garlic low and slow to get the best out of it – for at least 5 minutes. This will turn it from harsh and spicy to sweet and subtle.

Roasting: For an extra sweet, caramelised flavour, roast your garlic cloves whole in their skins with a generous amount of veg oil. Place them on a baking tray and roast for 30–45 minutes in an oven set to 180°C. This is a great way to add extra depth to curries (see the Roasted Tomato and Aubergine Curry on page 100).

GINGER

Preparing

In Indian cooking, ginger goes hand in hand with garlic and many hours of my life have been dedicated to prepping 'thumbs' of ginger for curry bases. Just like garlic, I have decided that my favourite way to prep ginger is by grating it. Again, a microplane works best but any old grater should do. Grating is far better at releasing ginger's juices than chopping.

Early on in my cooking career, I decided that life was far too short to waste time peeling ginger. Now I simply wash and grate. So far, no one has complained that they found a piece of ginger skin in their curry – I suspect they never will.

If you're working with a considerable amount of ginger, then another way of prepping it is by blitzing it in a blender with a splash of water. I only ever do this if cooking for more than six people – any less than that and it's simply not worth the washing up.

Most of my recipes call for a thumb-sized piece of ginger and, by this, I quite literally mean the size of a thumb – if you're lucky enough to have a thumb, you can use it to measure. For anyone else, this is roughly 5.5cm long and 1.5cm thick.

Cooking

Like garlic, raw ginger has a spicy, strong flavour but when cooked this subsides to a sweet, fresh, almost citrusy note. I therefore usually add ginger to the pan at the start of cooking, just after the onions and often with garlic.

GREEN BEANS

Preparing

Some people will tell you to top and tail your beans. I think this is a waste of time and bean. You just need to trim one side – the end with the woody stalk. Then cut them in half.

Cooking

Blanching: Green beans only ever need to be blanched. Boiled beans lose their natural sweetness and crunch. Bring a pan of water to the boil and add 1 tablespoon of fine sea salt. Add the beans and boil for 1 minute, or until they've turned dark green. Drain immediately and either run under cold water or plunge into iced water to stop them from cooking further.

When adding green beans to a curry, I don't cook them first – I simply simmer them in the curry sauce, just before taking it off the heat, which achieves the same sweet crunchy texture as blanching them.

Stir-frying/sautéing: Add the beans to a lightly oiled, hot frying pan, sprinkle them with salt and fry on a high heat for a few minutes until they've turned a darker shade of green and have charred slightly in places. Auntie Dolly once told me that when cooking beans like this (for thorans, sabzis etc) you should always add sugar, so now I do just that – 1 teaspoon to be precise.

JACKFRUIT

I will never ask you to tackle a whole fresh jackfruit. They are spiky, smelly and difficult to find, unless, like me, you're lucky enough to live next to lots of great Asian supermarkets. Instead, opt for the tinned young green jackfruit which can now be found in most supermarkets and health food shops.

Jackfruit is a great meat substitute, thanks to its stringy texture but, if not prepared and cooked correctly, it will be bland and rubbery.

Preparing

Drain and rinse the tinned jackfruit. It will come out in triangles with a pip in the centre. Use your hands to tear up the pieces, pulling apart the soft stringy flesh and digging your thumbs into the tougher ends to break them up. It's fine to eat the pips – they will cook down and you won't notice them. Once it's prepped, it should resemble pulled pork.

Cooking

Sautéing: Coat the bottom of a frying pan with veg oil and get it smoking hot. Add the prepped jackfruit with a pinch of salt and sugar and fry until it gets nice and crispy (around 15 minutes). Add spices of your choosing – smoked paprika, chilli powder and ground turmeric work well.

Roasting: Place the prepared jackfruit in a bowl and add veg oil, salt, sugar and spices of your choosing (see above). Mix well and transfer to a baking tray. Roast in an oven set to at least 200°C (hotter if you can) until the jackfruit gets nice and crispy (roughly 15–20 minutes).

KALE

Preparing

Pinch the bottom of the kale stem between your thumb and finger, then run them up the stem – the leaves should fall away. Discard the stem or use it to make homemade veg stock (page 32). Any thinner stems can be thinly sliced and cooked with the kale. If your kale leaves are big, use a knife to roughly shred them.

Cooking

Blanching: Kale only needs to be blanched not boiled. Bring a pan of water to the boil and add 1 tablespoon of fine sea salt. Add the kale and boil for 1 minute, or until it's turned dark green. Drain well, using your hands to squeeze out any excess water. I always finish kale with a pinch of sea salt flakes and a squeeze of lemon.

When adding kale to curries, I prep it as above and throw it raw into the sauce to cook, just before taking the pan off the heat. It will only need a minute or so to wilt down.

Stir-frying/sautéing: This is my favourite way to cook kale. Add the prepped kale to a lightly oiled, hot frying pan, and sprinkle with salt. Fry on a high heat for a few minutes until it's turned a darker shade of green and begun to wilt down. Finish with a squeeze of lemon and take off the heat. You can add some garlic to the pan at the start and, if you're feeling adventurous, some chilli flakes too.

LEEKS

Like cabbages, I think leeks are underrated. When cooked right, they dissolve down into silky-soft sweet strands of deliciousness.

Preparing

Chances are your leek will be harbouring some mud between its layers. This isn't ideal but leeks are worth the effort of cleaning. Use a knife to slice down the outer layer of the leek and peel it away (use for homemade veg stock on page 32). Thinly slice the leek (if the top of the leek is a bit tough you can also discard or use for the veg stock). The easiest way to get rid of the mud is by placing the slices in a bowl of cold water. Leave them for a couple of minutes and any mud or grit will sink to the bottom. Use your hands to skim the leeks off the surface of the water, leaving the mud at the bottom. Give the washed leeks a good squeeze with your hands to get rid of any excess water.

Cooking

Stir-frying/sautéing: In my opinion, the only way to cook leeks is by frying them slowly with lots of veg oil and salt. Heat a generous amount of oil in a frying pan and add the leeks, followed by a large pinch of salt. Turn down the heat to low and cook for 15 minutes until the leeks are super-soft and sweet. Finish with a squeeze of lemon if you fancy.

LEMONS

Preparing

I don't want to insult you by telling you how to cut a lemon, but recent experiences with my flatmate and boyfriend have compelled me to make a note on this.

To my horror, when adding lemon to things, they'll cut it in half and simply squeeze the juice from the lemon half and then, because often the half has more juice than they need, they'll put the semi-squeezed half back in the fridge, masquerading as a full half-lemon, only for me to find out later that it's been robbed of half its juice. Now that's off my chest ...

When prepping a lemon, you want to cut it in quarters, lengthways. This will help you get the most juice out of it. If it's full of pips, place your hand under the lemon when squeezing to catch any pips. Simple.

LIMES

Preparing

The lemon saga explained above applies to limes in my house too. Prep exactly the same way as lemons but, because limes are expensive and slightly punchier than lemons, you should aim to get eight segments out of your lime (cut your quarters in half lengthways again).

HOWEVER, before you cut your limes, you should *always* roll them. Put the lime on a flat surface and press down hard on the lime, rolling it back and forth. This releases all the juice and essential oils from the lime and makes it easier to squeeze.

MUSHROOMS

There's no need to get bogged down over which type of mushroom you should use in your curries. Simply go for what you like. I'd encourage you to try different varieties though, as they are all so unique in flavour and texture. I usually opt for button mushrooms because they are the most affordable and widely available.

Preparing

If your mushrooms are a bit muddy, resist the temptation to wash them as this dilutes the flavour and makes them soggy. Use a pastry brush, your hands or a piece of damp kitchen paper to rub the mud off.

Most of the time, I simply slice mushrooms in half. I leave small mushrooms whole.

Cooking

Stir-frying/sautéing: Always cook mushrooms on a high heat in a well-oiled frying pan with a generous pinch of salt. Fry until they have softened and caramelised – this will take around 10 minutes. Just before you take them off the heat, add a squeeze of lemon. I often throw in some chopped parsley at this stage too.

ONIONS

I've said it before and I'll say it again, the secret to a great curry is in the cooking of the onions. Generally speaking, I use red onions for tomato-based curries and white for coconut-based ones.

If I'm feeling fancy, I swap out onions for shallots, usually banana shallots as I find them easier to peel. Shallots are essentially mini onions with a milder, sweeter flavour –almost a hybrid of a red and white onion, pale in colour and sweet in flavour. Shallots are so, so good crisped up and sprinkled over rice dishes and dhals (see below for how to make these).

Preparing

About 90% of the time, I peel my onions and slice them into half-moons. To do this, stand the onion upright and cut it in half down the middle, then peel away the skin. Place it flat-side down on a chopping board and thinly slice it into little half-moon shapes.

Cooking

Frying: Always add salt to your onions at the start of cooking – this helps to draw out the moisture and get them super-soft and caramelised. It also helps to season the dish from the get-go. For a curry for four people, I usually add 1 teaspoon of fine sea salt. Be patient when cooking your onions – they will take at least 10–15 minutes to cook down on a low heat.

Crispy shallots: When making 'crispy onions' to garnish a dish, I use shallots as I find they crisp up easier. Peel and thinly slice your shallots – they need to be super-thin but a similar width so they cook evenly. Coat the bottom of a heavy-based frying pan with veg oil and put the shallots in the oil at room temperature. Turn the heat up to high – as the oil warms, the shallots will begin to bubble, this is the moisture evaporating off them. Don't stir the shallots – the more you leave them to do their thing, the crispier they will become. Once the bubbles have subsided, this means the moisture has cooked off. By this stage they should be golden brown. Use a slotted spoon to remove them from the oil and place them on a plate lined with kitchen paper. Sprinkle them with fine sea salt and leave to cool completely. They will get crispier as they cool.

PEAS

I feel slightly anxious if I don't have a bag of peas in my freezer. They work so well in curries, thrown in at the end to add sweet bursts of freshness. I'm too impatient to fiddle around with fresh peas.

Cooking

Frozen peas only need a tiny bit of cooking – you just want to defrost them. If you're adding them to a curry, add them right at the end, simmer for a minute or so until they're warmed through and then take the pan off the heat.

POTATOES

I have very strong opinions on how potatoes should be cooked …

Preparing

If they're muddy, wash them by soaking them in cold water and then scrubbing away any stubborn dirt. Don't bother peeling them – waste of time, waste of potato.

Cooking

Boiling: This is my favourite way to cook a potato – but only if the method is followed meticulously. Place the whole unpeeled potatoes in a large saucepan and cover them with cold water. Add at least 2 tablespoons of fine sea salt – the water should taste as salty as the sea. Bring the water to a rapid boil and cook. The cooking times will really vary depending on the size and variety of your potatoes, but you want to get your potatoes really soft, which will take at least 20 minutes for small and 40 minutes for medium-large potatoes. Once the skin begins to crack, you can check if they're ready by poking them with a fork – it should slide through really easily. I think a boiled potato should almost be falling apart once it's cooked.

Once your potatoes are at this stage, drain them in a colander and leave them to steam-dry for a few minutes. The skins should have a hint of a pale salty

crust and the insides should be light and fluffy. If you salted your water properly, they will be perfectly seasoned all the way through.

Roasting: I appreciate that there are many ways to roast a potato but this is the one I use most regularly and I think is the least amount of hassle. Cook your potatoes as above. While they are steam-drying, coat the bottom of a deep roasting tin with veg oil and place it in a really hot oven (200°C minimum). When your potatoes are dry and cool enough to handle, roughly chop them into halves and quarters (depending on the size) – keep all the small bits that have broken away. Add them to the roasting tin – the oil should be smoking hot by now. Roast for about 30 minutes until they're nice and crispy on the outside. Add a pinch of sea salt flakes and a dash of vinegar just before serving.

PUMPKiNS & SQUASHES

I love, love, love eating roasted pumpkin and squash in the winter and they make for such a great meat replacement in curries. There are so many varieties and I encourage you to get adventurous at your local farmers' market to find your own favourites. For the record, mine are acorn and onion squashes.

Preparing

My preferred way of cooking pumpkins and squash is roasting them whole. I find it so much easier to get the pips and stringy flesh out once they're cooked – just cut them in half and use a spoon to scoop it all out.

However, whole-roasting very large pumpkins or squash can lead to uneven cooking and super-soft flesh. Although there's nothing wrong with this in my opinion, some dishes, especially curries, require a bit more body (such as Rogan Squash on page 77). In this situation, I cut the pumpkin or squash in half with a big knife and scoop out the seeds. I then chop it up into 2.5cm chunks and roast (see opposite).

I never ever peel a pumpkin or squash. The skin goes so delicious and crispy when it's roasted and has so much flavour. Even if you're not roasting it, there's no need to peel.

Cooking

Roasting: Place the chunks in a roasting tin, drizzle with veg oil and add a generous pinch of fine sea salt. Shake the tray so the chunks get evenly coated. Roast in an oven set to 200°C for 30–40 minutes until the flesh is soft and the skin is golden brown.

Roasting whole: Place the whole squash in a roasting tin, drizzle with veg oil and add a generous pinch of fine sea salt. Use your hands to massage the salt and oil into the skin. Roast in an oven set to 200°C for 20–30 minutes until the flesh is soft and the skin is golden brown. You can test to see if it's ready by poking it with a knife – it should slide easily through.

SPiNACH

Preparing

If you're using large leaf spinach (my personal favourite), then you will need to wash and drain it before roughly shredding it with a knife. If using the smaller leaf stuff from a supermarket, you can add it straight from the bag.

Cooking

Stir-frying/sautéing: This is the only way I cook spinach. Heat a drizzle of veg oil in a frying pan and add the spinach. If it doesn't all fit, do this in stages. Season well with salt and pepper and stir until it wilts down. Finish with a squeeze of lemon and grating of nutmeg if you have some.

When adding spinach to curries, throw it in at the end and stir until it wilts down. Finish it off with a squeeze of lemon.

SWEET POTATO

Preparing

I think sweet potato works best cut into 2.5cm pieces and roasted. Surprise, surprise, I never peel them. You can also roast them whole but they go a lot softer so aren't great for curries.

Cooking

Roasting: Drizzle the chunks of sweet potato with veg oil, add a generous sprinkling of salt and roast in an oven set at 180°C for 25–30 minutes until soft in the middle and crispy on the outside.

Roasting whole: Place on a baking tray and roast in an oven set at 180°C for about 45 minutes until soft in the middle and crispy on the outside.

Cooking in curries: Sweet potato takes a surprisingly short time to cook so I often add them to curries raw – just make sure there's enough sauce to cook them in. Put the chunks of sweet potato in the sauce, cover with a lid and simmer for around 25 minutes until soft.

TOMATOES

Tomatoes are a key ingredient in many Indian dishes. Sadly, here in the UK, it's always a gamble whether your tomatoes will be sweet and juicy or hard and bland but I find that adding sugar with tomatoes helps to spruce up even the saddest specimens.

Proper tomatoes have a glorious balance of sweet and sour. The sugar helps bring out the natural sweetness and, if this isn't enough, a glug of vinegar can really take things up a level. So, there you have it, the secret to a great-tasting tomato-based dish is a spoonful of sugar and a glug of vinegar.

Preparing

When using whole tomatoes, most of my recipes ask you to 'roughly dice them'. By this I mean simply cutting them up into chunks about 1cm by 1cm. I will never ask you to deseed or peel a tomato.

Cooking

Sautéing: As explained opposite, after adding fresh tomatoes to a pan, I follow them with a pinch of salt, a teaspoon of sugar and often a small splash of red wine vinegar. If you're using tomato purée, leave out the salt and vinegar as it's already quite punchy and just needs a touch of sweetness. Tinned tomatoes vary hugely in quality. If you're working with the basics range, use the sugar and vinegar trick. If you've gone luxe, you probably won't need it.

Roasting: Another way to bring out the sweetness in tomatoes is by roasting them. Preheat your oven to 180°C. Place the tomatoes on a roasting tray and drizzle with veg oil and add a generous pinch of salt. Make sure you keep any vines on the tomato as this helps boost the flavour. Roast for 25 minutes or until the tomatoes are starting to melt down into the tray. From here you can add them straight to a frying pan in place of tinned tomatoes or passata (around 12 medium vine tomatoes should be a good sub for a tin of chopped tomatoes).

Passata vs tinned tomatoes: Some of my recipes call for passata rather than tinned tomatoes – this is simply blended tomatoes but I think it has a slightly sweeter note. Passata is totally interchangeable with tinned tomatoes, you may just need to add a bit more water as it tends to be thicker.

HOMEMADE VEG STOCK

I really hate wasting food and, over the years, have come up with tips and tricks to make sure that as little food as possible ends up in my compost bin. This includes storing fresh herbs in glasses of water in my fridge (they can last up to a month like this), making sure I don't peel veg unless absolutely necessary, and making stock with leftover vegetable trimmings.

There isn't really a recipe for homemade veg stock per se as the veg you have to hand will vary depending on what you've been cooking. I tend to make mine after I've cooked a big meal for lots of people – while cooking, I'll make a bag full of trimmings such as onion skins, garlic skins, cauliflower leaves, the outer leaves of leeks, the stalks of thyme, parsley, coriander and kale, lemon skins and apple cores. You get the idea – nothing escapes my broth. Some will tell you not to add starchy veg such as potato and squash skins as it will turn your stock cloudy and a bit thick, but I don't see an issue with this.

To make the stock, put your trimmings in a large, deep saucepan and cover them with water. Add a generous pinch of salt, a handful of peppercorns, perhaps one or two star anise, or any other whole spices you have lying around (I love adding fennel seeds too). Bring the pan to the boil, then turn the heat down to very low and simmer for at least an hour. The longer you simmer, the more concentrated the flavour. Drain the broth over a colander and store in the fridge for up to five days (or in the freezer for up to six months) until you need it to make some pilau rice, a curry or soup.

OTHER KEY INGREDIENTS

I have tried to ensure that the recipes in this book are accessible to most home cooks and have therefore attempted to avoid difficult-to-find ingredients. Below I've listed a few ingredients, which will be probably be familiar to you already but that will really elevate your curry game.

Chillies

There are hundreds of different varieties of chilli, but for the recipes in this book you only need to know about three.

Green chillies

This is the type of chilli I use most in my cooking. I use thin green 'Kenyan' chillies which can be found in Asian stores or greengrocers. These have a lovely fresh taste and an initial punch of spice which subsides quickly. I often just slit the chillies lengthways down the middle which helps release their flavour without unleashing all the heat.

Dried red chillies

When toasted in hot oil, dried red chillies have a gorgeous nutty flavour. If you add these chillies in whole, they will release the least heat. You can adjust the level of heat by tearing the chilli before you put it in the pan and shaking out the seeds. The more you rip it up, the more seeds will be released and the spicier the dish will be. These chillies have a punchier kick to them, which builds over a period of time and lingers longer than a green chilli.

You can buy Indian dried red chillies from Indian shops or online. I use the TRS brand's 'Whole Red Chillies' – make sure you don't get the 'extra hot' ones as they will blow your head off!

Another form of dried red chillies are Kashmiri chillies – these have far less heat and a slightly sweeter but still nutty flavour. They are perfect if you want just a hint of spice but the flavour of chilli. Again, these are available from Indian shops and online.

Chilli flakes

If you can't find whole dried chillies, chilli flakes are a great alternative. They also add a lovely fleck of colour to dishes. I often use chilli flakes as a garnish, for some quick spice and colour. They have a good kick of heat and, when fried in oil, the same nutty flavour as whole dried chillies. They are available in all supermarkets.

Spices

Almost every spice listed in the book can be easily found in UK supermarkets. If you're new to curry cooking, I suggest that you start by stocking up on these basic spices: ground turmeric, ground coriander, ground cumin, cumin seeds and chilli powder. With these five spices, you will be able to cook many of the recipes that follow. If you don't have a certain spice to hand, please don't panic – it's not the end of the world if you have to leave it out or sub it for a different one. In fact, this experimentation will help to boost your confidence and begin to teach you how to build your own curry recipes.

Salt

I am extremely passionate about the importance of salt in cooking. It is hands down the most used ingredient in my kitchen. I really do believe that the difference between an average cook and a great cook is the art of using salt properly.

Dishes need to be seasoned at every stage of cooking – a handful in the water you boil your potatoes in, a generous pinch once you've added your onions to the pan, a sprinkling after you've torn in the spinach and a final dash once the dish is ready.

The rise of processed food, 'hidden salt' and traffic light warning symbols on food packaging have led to

salt being villainised in modern society. However, if you're cooking your food from scratch, you can afford to be generous with the salt.

Sea salt vs table salt

All my recipes call for sea salt rather than table salt. Table salt is processed and has additives that give it a metallic taste. It's also *really* salty – so if you're using table salt you will need to reduce the quantities stated in the recipe.

Sea salt comes in many varieties. When cooking, I tend to use fine sea salt but I always have a pot of Maldon sea salt flakes next to my cooker for finishing dishes. However, they are far too expensive to use for seasoning water and curry sauces, so make sure you always have a big tub of the fine stuff to hand.

Curry leaves

If you can, I implore you to seek out fresh curry leaves. They can be found in most Asian shops and online – Waitrose and Ocado even stock them now. Stock up on them when you find them and put what you don't need in the freezer. Curry leaves will take your Indian cooking to the next level, adding a really authentic flavour to your dishes – they have a gorgeous, fragrant, citrusy flavour, and when fried release a nutty aroma. When adding the leaves, you can also throw in the woody stalks as these will add an extra boost of flavour – just make sure you pick them out before serving.

If you can't find fresh curry leaves, don't bother with the dried leaves – they're a waste of money and your dish will be better without them.

Coconut milk

Coconut milk varies hugely in quality – always check the percentage of coconut on the tin. Never opt for anything lower than 50%. My favourite brand to cook with is Chaokoh. *Never ever* use low-fat coconut milk.

Cooking oil

Almost all my recipes call for 'veg oil', and by this I mean sunflower or rapeseed oil. These are both neutral in flavour, widely available and affordable.

If I had to choose between the two, rapeseed would be my preferred choice.

Some recipes do specify coconut oil – for a touch more flavour. When buying coconut oil, look for the unrefined virgin stuff as it has a more coconutty flavour. Annoyingly, it is quite pricey but it can always be subbed out for veg oil.

Cinnamon sticks

I use cassia bark when cooking curries, as it has a strong cinnamon taste without the sweetness of a cinnamon quill. It is also far more economical. You can find it in most Asian shops and online.

Garam masala

Garam masala is a blend of ground spices used to season dishes. No blend is identical – every Indian region, family and person will have their own unique blend of spices that they use. The common themes tend to be cumin, coriander, black pepper, fennel, cinnamon and cardamom.

Garam masala is usually used towards the end of cooking, similar to how you might use pepper to season a dish. It will add a new dimension to your cooking, tying up a dish with an extra-fragrant layer of spicing.

Garam masala blends can be found at most supermarkets. You can also make your own – there are plenty of recipes online.

Nuts, seeds and coconut flakes

It is sacrilege to eat untoasted nuts and seeds. Roasting nuts and seeds basically gets the most out of them – it releases their essential oils, bringing out all those nutty flavours, and gives them extra crunch.

Place any nuts or seeds on a baking tray and roast them in an oven set to 150°C for around 15 minutes until they're a light golden-brown. Allow them to cool before eating – this stage is essential for the crunch.

If you're in a hurry, you can also toast nuts and seeds in a hot, dry frying pan, tossing regularly until golden.

The same rules apply to coconut flakes. I usually toast these in a hot, dry frying pan until golden.

KiTCHEN EQUiPMENT

You really don't need fancy cooking equipment to make a great meal. The list below will help you cook the recipes in this book. I have also included some easy substitutes you can make if you don't have what's called for.

Frying pan

I cook most curries in a large, deep, heavy-based frying pan, with a lid. If you don't have one, a wok works well. I find a large roasting tin works well as a makeshift lid.

Casserole dish

Some recipes in this book call for a shallow, cast-iron casserole dish. These are better for slow cooking than a standard frying pan as they are thick and evenly disperse heat. If you don't have one, an ovenproof frying pan and lid will work.

Saucepan

Any will do. I always lose my saucepan lids and often end up using plates as lids – they work pretty well.

Spatula

A wooden spatula is the perfect utensil for stirring curries. A wooden spoon will also do!

Blender

I have a small 650ml Ninja blender in my kitchen which works for pretty much anything – such as grinding spices, blending onions, garlic and ginger, or making cashew cream. I really recommend getting one if you plan to do lots of Indian cooking. If you don't have one, coffee grinders make for great spice grinders, as do pestles and mortars. Handheld stick blenders will work for onion, garlic and ginger, chutneys, sauces and cashew cream.

Fine microplane

This is what I use to grate garlic and ginger. It is *so* worth the investment. If you don't have one, see the notes under 'garlic' on page 21.

Teaspoons and tablespoons

All measurements in this book are based on measuring spoons rather than domestic teaspoons and tablespoons, which vary in size. You are more than welcome to use your own teaspoons etc, as long as you keep tasting the dish, as the quantities of spices and salt may need to change.

CURRIES

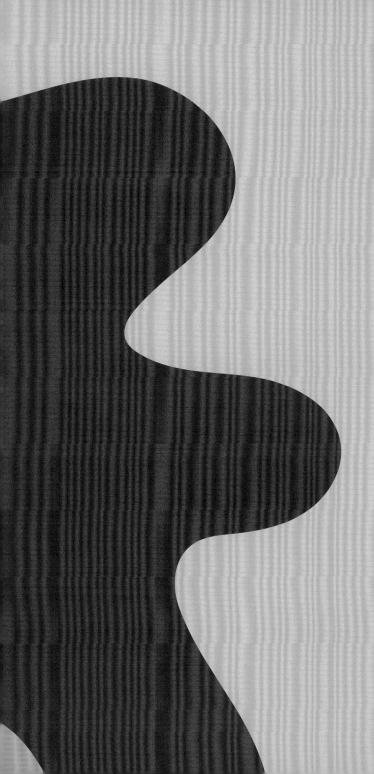

The word curry derives from the Tamil word kari, which means 'sauce' or 'relish for rice'. While curries come in many different forms, in the West we've come to think of a curry as that steaming bowl of meat, fish or veg doused in a fragrant sauce, often tomato- or coconut-based, and rich with spices.

These are the Indian dishes that us Brits have fallen in love with and passionately embraced as part of our own food culture. For me, this is where food has a powerful role to play in the meeting of different cultures. We must tread this ground carefully, however, and not blindly appropriate another country's cuisine, claiming it as our own, but instead show deep love and respect for the food of our sub-continental neighbours. We are so lucky to have such accessible Indian food available to us on pretty much every high street in the UK. Long live the Great British Curry House!

THE BASE RECIPES

Broadly speaking, you can sort curries into two categories: tomato-based and coconut-based. The following two base recipes are the building blocks for great curries.

Almost all curries are built around the principle of frying onions, garlic, ginger, chilli and a triumvirate of spices – cumin, coriander and turmeric. From here, you either go down the tomato route – rich, sweet and sour with deep notes of earthy spices; or the coconut route – creamy, fragrant and fresh. The difference between a good curry base and a great one is the cooking of the onions and the use of salt. You want to cook onions down for as long as possible with a generous amount of salt from the start. Red onions add an extra dimension of sweetness, which is great for tomato bases, and white onions suit coconut bases as they don't colour the sauce.

If you are a prolific curry cooker, then I suggest doubling the following recipes, portioning them up and freezing them to whip out as and when the curry night craving hits. See the 'Pimp Your Base' section for ideas on how to turn these recipes into different curries.

COCONUT CURRY BASE

Serves 4

3 tbsp veg oil
1 tsp cumin seeds
1 tsp brown mustard seeds
3 cardamom pods, crushed
10 fresh curry leaves or
    2 bay leaves
1 large white onion, sliced
1 green chilli, slit lengthways
4 large garlic cloves, grated
    or crushed
A thumb-sized piece of ginger,
    grated
1 tsp ground coriander
½ tsp ground turmeric
1 tsp sugar
1 × 400ml tin of coconut milk
Juice of ¼ lemon
Salt

Heat the oil in a large frying pan on a medium heat and add the cumin seeds, mustard seeds and cardamom pods. Fry until the seeds begin to pop, then add the curry or bay leaves. When the leaves begin to crisp up, add the onion and 1 teaspoon of salt, then turn the heat down low to cook the onion really slowly. When the onion begins to soften – after about 5 minutes – add the chilli, garlic and ginger, and cook until the onion is completely soft and caramelised (10–15 minutes in total).

Add the coriander, turmeric and sugar. Stir-fry for a couple of minutes, then add the coconut milk. Fill the empty tin a quarter full with water and rinse it out into the pan. Turn the heat up to bring the pan to a simmer, then let it cook on low for 5 minutes until the sauce has reduced slightly. Add the lemon juice and taste for seasoning.

TOMATO CURRY BASE

Serves 4

3 tbsp veg oil
2 tsp cumin seeds
1 cassia bark or cinnamon stick
2 bay leaves
1 large red onion, sliced into
    half-moons
4 large garlic cloves, grated
    or crushed
A thumb-sized piece of ginger,
    grated
1 tsp chilli flakes
1 tsp ground coriander
1 tsp ground cumin
½ tsp ground turmeric
1 tsp paprika
2 tbsp tomato purée
2 tsp sugar
1 tbsp red wine vinegar
1 × 400g tin of chopped tomatoes
    or passata
1 tsp garam masala
Salt

Heat the oil in a large frying pan on a medium heat and add the cumin seeds, cassia bark or cinnamon stick and bay leaves. Fry until the seeds are golden and aromatic. Add the onion and 1 teaspoon of salt, then turn the heat down low to cook the onion really slowly. When the onion begins to soften – after about 5 minutes – add the garlic and ginger, and cook until the onion is completely soft and caramelised (10–15 minutes in total).

Add the chilli flakes, coriander, cumin, turmeric and paprika. Stir-fry for a couple of minutes, then add the tomato purée and sugar. Cook for 2 minutes until the purée has turned a darker shade of red, then add the vinegar followed by the tomatoes or passata. Fill the empty tin or bottle with water and rinse it out into the pan. Turn the heat up to bring the pan to a simmer, then let it cook on low for 20 minutes until the sauce has reduced. Stir through the garam masala and taste for seasoning.

PiMP YOUR BASE

See pages 12–30 for tips on cooking vegetables.

Simple curry suggestions using the tomato base

Chickpea and sweet potato
Spinach and butternut squash
Roasted cauliflower, chickpea and spinach
Kale and potato
Pea and aubergine

Simple curry suggestions using the coconut base

Broccoli, kale and peas
Potato, peas and green beans
Kale and sweet potato
Aubergine, tomato and sugar snap peas
Courgette, new potato and peas

CASHEW & COCONUT KORMA

This is probably the most popular dish in the curry house and has been on the menu since the days when I was cooking all the curries in my home kitchen. I served it up for my boyfriend at the time (a professional curry taster by this point) and, as he started to eat it, he went silent. Once the bowl had been scraped clean, he looked up at me and told me it was the best curry I'd ever made. So, I knew I was on to a winner.

Feel free to switch up the veg for whatever's in season. I find this curry works best with one starchy vegetable and a mix of two or three fresher, green veg to cut through the creaminess.

Serves 4

120g cashew nuts, plus a few to garnish
½ large butternut squash, cut into 2.5cm chunks
3 tbsp veg oil, plus extra for roasting the squash
1 tsp cumin seeds
2 cloves
3 cardamom pods, crushed
2 bay leaves
1 medium white onion, sliced into half-moons
4 large garlic cloves, crushed
A thumb-sized piece of ginger, grated
1 green chilli, slit lengthways
1 tsp fenugreek seeds
1 small head of broccoli, cut into florets
½ tsp ground turmeric
1 tsp sugar
1 × 400ml tin of coconut milk
100g green beans, topped and cut in half
A handful of frozen peas
1½ limes, 1 quartered, to garnish
Salt

Cover the cashews with cold water and leave to soak for at least 2 hours.

Preheat the oven to 200°C. Place the chunks of squash in a roasting tin, drizzle with veg oil and add a generous pinch of salt. Shake the tray so the chunks get evenly coated. Roast for 30–40 minutes, until the flesh is soft and the skin is golden brown. Set aside until ready to use.

Heat the oil in a large frying pan on a medium heat and add the cumin seeds, cloves, cardamom pods and bay leaves. Fry until the seeds are golden and aromatic. Add the onion and 1 teaspoon of salt and turn the heat down low to cook the onion really slowly. When the onion begins to soften – after about 5 minutes – add the garlic, ginger, chilli and fenugreek seeds, and cook until the onion is completely soft and caramelised (10–15 minutes in total).

Turn up the heat and add the broccoli, the turmeric and the sugar, followed by a pinch of salt. Stir-fry for a couple of minutes until the broccoli is well coated with the onion mix and then pour in the coconut milk. Turn down the heat and simmer for 5 minutes until the broccoli is cooked through but still has some bite.

While the broccoli cooks, make the cashew cream. Drain the cashews and tip into a blender. Pour in 80ml cold water and blitz until a smooth cream is formed. Add the cream to the pan, along with the roasted squash and the green beans, and cover the pan with a lid.

While the beans cook, heat a small, dry frying pan on a medium heat and toast the leftover cashews until golden brown. Set these aside.

Add the frozen peas and allow them to cook through, then take the pan off the heat and stir through the juice of ½ lime. Taste for seasoning. Serve in a bowl, topped with the toasted cashews and a wedge of lime.

BUTTERBEAN, SQUASH & SPiNACH COCONUT CURRY

This curry will become your winter weekday stalwart – warming, nutritious and not too heavy. Once you've made it, you'll never know how you lived without it. Make extra – it will keep in your fridge for up to a week, and freezes well.

Serves 2

½ large butternut squash, cut into
    2.5cm chunks
3 tbsp veg oil, plus extra for
    roasting the squash
1 tsp cumin seeds
1 tsp brown mustard seeds
1 tsp fennel seeds
1 medium white onion, sliced into
    half-moons
1 tsp sugar
4 garlic cloves, grated or crushed
A thumb-sized piece of ginger,
    grated
1 green chilli, slit lengthways
1 tsp ground coriander
1 tsp ground cumin
2 tsp curry powder
1 × 400g tin of butter beans,
    rinsed and drained
1 × 400ml tin of coconut milk
2 large handfuls of spinach
Juice of ½ lemon
Salt

Preheat the oven to 200°C.

Place the chunks of squash in a roasting tin, drizzle with veg oil and add a generous pinch of salt. Shake the tray so the chunks get evenly coated. Roast for 30–40 minute, until the flesh is soft and the skin is golden brown. Set aside until ready to use.

Heat the oil in a large frying pan on a medium heat and add the cumin, mustard and fennel seeds. Fry until the seeds begin to pop. Add the onion, 1 teaspoon of salt and the sugar, and turn the heat down low to cook the onion really slowly. When it begins to soften – after about 5 minutes – add the garlic, ginger and chilli, and cook until the onion is completely soft and caramelised (10–15 minutes in total).

Add the ground coriander, cumin and curry powder, and stir-fry for a couple of minutes. Turn the heat up to medium, add the butter beans and roasted squash, and stir to coat them with the onion mix. Pour the coconut milk into the pan. Fill the empty tin a quarter full with water and rinse it out into the pan. Bring the pan to a simmer, then let it cook on low for 15 minutes or until the sauce has reduced a little. Add the spinach and stir until it has all wilted. Take the pan off the heat and add the lemon juice. Taste for seasoning.

CAULi TiKKA MASALA

This recipe is an homage to the curry-house favourite, rather than being a carbon copy. You'll find that it's more fragrant and lighter than the sweet, rich, creamy curry you find on high streets up and down the UK.

The cauliflower is roasted in the tikka marinade so it becomes smoky and almost meaty, providing the perfect substitute for chicken.

Serves 4

For the cauli tikka marinade
130g plain unsweetened soya yoghurt (I use Alpro)
4 large garlic cloves, grated or crushed
A thumb-sized piece of ginger, grated
1 tbsp smoked paprika
1 tbsp curry powder
1 tsp chilli powder
½ tsp ground turmeric
½ tbsp ground cumin
½ tbsp ground coriander
1 tsp fine sea salt
Juice of ½ lemon
1 medium cauliflower, cut into florets (discard the tough outer leaves but keep the soft inner ones)
Veg oil

Ingredients cont. page 56

Preheat the oven to 220°C.

Start by making the cauli tikka. Mix all the marinade ingredients in a bowl (except the veg oil) and add the cauliflower. Stir until it's completely coated and then place on an oiled baking tray, keeping some leaves back. Drizzle some more oil over the top of the cauli. Bake in the oven for 25–30 minutes or until golden on the outside and soft in the middle. Halfway through cooking, take the tray out to give it a stir and add the cauli leaves you held back.

Recipe cont. page 56

For the curry sauce

4 tbsp veg oil

2 bay leaves

3 cardamom pods, crushed

A medium bunch of coriander, roughly chopped (stalks included)

1 medium red onion, roughly chopped

4 garlic cloves, roughly chopped

A thumb-sized piece of ginger, roughly chopped

1 tsp fenugreek seeds

1 tbsp tomato purée

1 tsp sugar

1 tsp ground cumin

1 tsp ground coriander

1 tsp chilli powder

1 × 400g tin of chopped tomatoes

1 large green pepper, deseeded and cut into 1.5cm chunks

1 × 400ml tin of coconut milk

Juice of ½ lemon

Salt

While the cauliflower roasts, make the curry sauce.

Heat 3 tablespoons of oil in a large frying pan on a medium heat and add the bay leaves and cardamom pods. Fry until golden and aromatic, and then add half the chopped coriander – watch out as the oil will spit. Add the red onion and 1 teaspoon of salt, stir and turn the heat down low to cook the onion really slowly. When the onion begins to soften – after about 5 minutes – add the garlic, ginger and fenugreek seeds, and cook until the onion is completely soft and caramelised (10–15 minutes in total).

Add the tomato purée, sugar, ground cumin, ground coriander and chilli powder, and stir-fry for a few minutes until the purée has turned a darker shade of red. Stir through the chopped tomatoes and take off the heat. Transfer the mix to a blender (or use a stick blender) and blitz until you have a smooth sauce.

Wipe down the frying pan and place it back on a medium heat. Add the remaining 1 tablespoon of oil and when it is hot add the green pepper. Fry until it begins to colour. Pour the tomato sauce back into the pan and bring to a simmer. Stir through the coconut milk to heat through.

By this time, the cauliflower should be roasted. Take it out of the oven and add it to the pan. When everything is well combined, take the pan off the heat and stir through the lemon juice and remaining chopped coriander. Taste for seasoning.

SWEET POTATO & BROCCOLI MADRAS

The madras is a British curry-house favourite thanks to its punchy spice and flavour. I find that adding a few spoonfuls of mango chutney at the end really helps balance all the flavours and tame the heat a little.

Serves 4

1 medium sweet potato, cut into 2.5cm chunks (skin on)

3 tbsp veg oil, plus extra for roasting the sweet potato

3 cardamom pods, crushed

2 dried red chillies, ripped into thirds

A small bunch of coriander, roughly chopped (stalks included)

1 red onion, sliced into half-moons

4 large garlic cloves, grated or crushed

A thumb-sized piece of ginger, grated

4 green chillies, 2 slit lengthways and 2 finely chopped, to garnish

1 tbsp tomato purée

1 tsp sugar

1 tsp ground cumin

1 tsp ground coriander

1 tsp chilli powder

1 tbsp madras curry powder

½ tsp ground turmeric

200g broccoli, cut into small florets

1 × 400g tin of chopped tomatoes

2 tbsp mango chutney

1 tsp garam masala

Juice of ½ lemon

Salt

Preheat the oven to 180°C.

Place the sweet potato on a baking tray, drizzle with oil and sprinkle with a generous pinch of salt. Roast in the oven for 25–30 minutes until it's soft and crispy in places.

While your sweet potato roasts, heat the oil in a large frying pan on a medium heat and add the cardamom pods. Fry until golden and aromatic, then add the dried red chillies and coriander – watch out for spitting oil. Cook until the coriander leaves turn a darker shade of green, this will only take a couple of minutes.

Add the onion and 1 teaspoon of salt and turn the heat down low to cook the onion really slowly. When the onion begins to soften – after about 5 minutes – add the garlic, ginger and 2 whole green chillies, and cook until the onion is completely soft and caramelised (10–15 minutes in total).

Add the tomato purée, sugar, ground cumin, ground coriander, chilli powder, curry powder and turmeric, and stir-fry for a few minutes until the purée has turned a darker shade of red. Turn up the heat, add the broccoli and fry for a couple of minutes until it has turned a darker shade of green.

Add the chopped tomatoes to the pan, fill the empty tin with water and rinse it out into the pan. Add the roasted sweet potato and mango chutney, and bring it up to a simmer. Stir through the garam masala and continue to cook for 5 minutes, or until the sauce has reduced slightly. Take the pan off the heat and add the lemon juice. Taste for seasoning.

Garnish with the chopped green chillies to serve.

SPRING VEG COCONUT CURRY

I love spring. Not only does the sun begin to shine again, but the selection of British vegetables on offer starts to widen. By April, I'm pretty kale, squash and potato-ed out and I begin counting down the days until I can bite into a sweet, crunchy sugar snap pea, green bean or pink radish.

If you find yourself with a glut of green spring veg, this is the curry for you. The creamy, fragrant coconut sauce is the perfect carrier for the fresh greens. For tips on preparing and cooking all vegetables, see pages 12–30.

Serves 4

150g new potatoes
1 tbsp coconut oil
1 tsp brown mustard seeds
1 tsp cumin seeds
1 tsp fennel seeds
1 large white onion, sliced into
  half-moons
1 tsp sugar
1 green chilli, slit lengthways
10 fresh curry leaves (optional,
  leave out if you can't find fresh)
4 large garlic cloves, grated or
  crushed
A thumb-sized piece of ginger,
  grated
1 tsp ground coriander
½ tsp ground turmeric
100g green beans, topped and
  cut in half
A handful of sugar snap peas
1 large courgette, sliced into
  half-moons
1 × 400ml tin of coconut milk
A handful of frozen peas
Juice of ½ lemon
Salt

Fill a large saucepan with water and add 2 tablespoons of salt. Add the potatoes whole (don't peel them!) and bring to the boil. Cook until they are nice and soft – small new potatoes will take at least 20 minutes from cold but it will depend on their size. Once the skin begins to crack, test if they're ready by poking them with a fork – it should slide very easily into the potatoes. Drain and leave to steam-dry in a colander. When they are cool enough to handle, break them in half with your hands.

Heat the oil in a large frying pan on a medium heat and add the mustard, cumin and fennel seeds. When they begin to pop, add the onion, 1 teaspoon of salt and the sugar, and turn the heat down low to cook the onion really slowly. When the onion begins to soften – after about 5 minutes – add the chilli, curry leaves, garlic, ginger and ground coriander, and cook until the onion is completely soft and caramelised (10–15 minutes in total).

Add the turmeric and all the veg, apart from the peas. Stir-fry for a few minutes, then add the coconut milk, along with a splash of water if needed. Turn the heat up to bring the pan to a simmer, then let it cook on low for 10 minutes. Add the peas and stir until they are cooked through. Take the pan off the heat and add the lemon juice. Taste for seasoning.

SMOKY AUBERGINE & PEA CURRY

This smoky aubergine curry was on the menu when I was still cooking in my home kitchen. It turned out that smoking a box of aubergines on my domestic gas hob was quite a task – on the days I'd cook this curry, my kitchen would turn into a smoky curry hotbox! But it was worth it for the flavour. Traditionally, this Punjabi dish would call for the aubergines to be smoked over charcoal and, if you're cooking this in the summer with a coal BBQ to hand, I'd definitely recommend this method (see page 12 for instructions). However, if you have a gas hob, then cooking the aubergines over the flame works almost as well – and I've included that method here. If you don't have a gas hob or a BBQ, you can roast the aubergine and add the smoked paprika and – if you can get your hands on some – liquid smoke (a food flavouring you can usually find online).

Serves 4

4 large aubergines

Ingredients cont. page 62

Start by cooking the aubergines – smoking them on a gas hob (or BBQ) if you can. If you don't want to get your hob dirty, you can put down some foil around the rings. Pierce the aubergines all over with a fork and use tongs to sit them on top of a low flame from a medium ring. Leave for 5 minutes until the skin is completely charred, then turn over so you can char the other side. Repeat until they are charred all the way around, and the skin is almost falling away from the soft middle. Place them in a colander over a bowl to cool down. When the aubergines are cool enough to handle, peel away the black skin with your hands and discard. Chop the flesh into chunks and set aside until you are ready to use it.

Recipe cont. page 62

150ml veg oil, plus extra if roasting
the aubergine
2 tsp cumin seeds
A medium bunch of coriander
(stalks included), roughly
chopped
2½ medium red onions, sliced
into half-moons (save the half
to garnish)
5 large garlic cloves, grated
or crushed
A thumb-sized piece of ginger,
grated
1 green chilli, slit lengthways
2 tbsp tomato purée
2 tsp sugar
4 medium tomatoes, roughly
chopped
1 tsp hot chilli powder
1 tsp ground coriander
1 tsp ground cumin
2 tsp smoked paprika
1 tsp liquid smoke (optional,
only use if you can't smoke
the aubergines)
3 large handfuls of frozen peas
Juice of ¼ lemon
Salt

If you can't smoke the aubergines, roast them. Preheat the oven to 180°C. Cut the aubergines into 2.5cm chunks, sprinkle them with salt and leave for 10 minutes. Drizzle evenly with a generous amount of veg oil and roast for 30–40 minutes until they're soft and caramelised.

To make the sauce, heat the oil in a large frying pan on a medium heat and add the cumin seeds and half the coriander – watch out for spitting oil. Fry until the coriander has turned a darker shade of green.

Add the onions and 1 teaspoon of salt, and turn the heat down low to cook the onions really slowly. When the onions begin to soften – after about 5 minutes – add the garlic, ginger and green chilli, and cook until the onion is completely soft and caramelised (10–15 minutes in total).

Add the tomato purée and sugar. Stir for a couple of minutes until it has turned a darker shade of red, then add the fresh tomatoes, followed by the ground spices, a splash of water and the liquid smoke (if using). Turn the heat up to bring the pan to a simmer, cover with a lid and leave to cook on a low heat for 10 minutes until the tomatoes have broken down into the onion mix and the oil has separated from the purée.

Add the cooked aubergine and peas, followed by a generous pinch of salt. Put a lid on the pan and simmer for 5 minutes. Take the pan off the heat and stir through the lemon juice and the other half of the coriander. Taste for seasoning. Serve topped with the red onion slices or the Pink Onion Pickle on page 228.

SWEET POTATO, SHALLOT & AUBERGINE BHUNA

A relatively recent addition to our curry-house menu is Soya Bhuna. It came about because we had a glut of soya chunks lying around and, while trying to come up with something to do with them, some of our chefs suggested the curry-house favourite: the bhuna. As soya chunks aren't ubiquitous in British supermarkets (and tend to divide opinion), here they've been swapped out for sweet potato and aubergine which soak up all this delicious sauce brilliantly. The shallots bring a sweet and sharp note, which pairs perfectly with the tomatoes.

Serves 4

1 medium sweet potato, cut into 2.5cm chunks (skin on)
250ml veg oil, plus extra for roasting the sweet potato
A large bunch of coriander, roughly chopped (stalks included)
4 banana shallots, cut in half lengthways
5 large garlic cloves, grated or crushed
A thumb-sized piece of ginger, grated
2 green chillies, slit lengthways
6 medium tomatoes, quartered
1 tsp fenugreek seeds
1 tsp smoked paprika
1 tsp chilli powder
1 tsp ground cumin
1 tsp ground coriander
2 tbsp tomato purée
1 tsp sugar
1 tbsp red wine vinegar
2 medium aubergines, cut into 2.5cm chunks
½ tsp ground turmeric
1 tsp garam masala
Salt

Preheat the oven to 180°C.

Place the sweet potato on a baking tray, drizzle with oil and sprinkle with a generous pinch of salt. Roast in the oven for 25–30 minutes until it's soft and crispy in places. Set aside until ready to use.

Heat the oil in a large frying pan on a medium heat and add half the fresh coriander – watch out for spitting oil. Once it has turned a darker shade of green and is smelling amazing (around 2 minutes), add the shallots flat-side down in the pan, followed by 1 teaspoon of salt. Turn down the heat to low and fry until they begin to caramelise on one side (around 15 minutes). Flip the shallots over, encouraging the strands apart with your spatula.

Add the garlic, ginger and green chillies, and cook with the shallots. The mix is ready when the smell of raw garlic has gone and the shallots are soft and caramelised (about another 10–15 minutes).

Turn up the heat and add the fresh tomatoes and the rest of the spices (apart from the turmeric and garam masala) and fry for a couple of minutes. Add the tomato purée, sugar, vinegar and 100ml water, and fry for a few minutes until the purée has turned a darker shade of red. Then add the aubergines, turmeric and a pinch of salt. Turn the heat down low, cover the pan with a lid and cook slowly until the aubergine is soft and almost melting into the sauce (around 20–30 minutes).

Remove the lid and add the cooked sweet potato and garam masala. Stir well and then add the rest of the chopped coriander. Taste for seasoning. Serve topped with the Pink Onion Pickle (page 228).

SPINACH & POTATO CURRY

The humble potato is not to be underestimated. In fact, it's one of my favourite vegetables. Yes, crisps and chips are delicious, but my favourite incarnation of the potato is a floury one (Maris Piper or King Edward), boiled in really salty water until it's almost falling apart. I'd happily eat these by themselves but, when cooked like this, they're such great flavour sponges that it would be rude not to put them in a curry sauce.

This curry is unapologetically simple – both a homage to the humble potato and a nod to the trusty curry-night side dish, saag aloo.

Serves 4

4 large floury potatoes (such as King Edward or Maris Piper)
3 tbsp veg oil
2 tsp cumin seeds
1 tsp brown mustard seeds
1 medium white onion, sliced into half-moons
4 large garlic cloves, grated or crushed
A thumb-sized piece of ginger, grated
1 green chilli, thinly sliced
2 tsp curry powder
3 medium tomatoes, roughly chopped
½ tsp ground turmeric
1 × 400ml tin of coconut milk
2 large handfuls of spinach
Juice of ½ lemon
Salt
A small bunch of coriander, roughly chopped (stalks included), to garnish

Fill a large saucepan with water and add at least 2 tablespoons of salt – it should taste as salty as the sea. Add the potatoes whole (don't peel them!) and bring to the boil. Cook until they are nice and soft – it will take at least 40 minutes from cold but will depend on size and variety. Once the skin begins to crack, test if they're ready by poking them with a fork – it should slide very easily into the potatoes. Drain and leave to steam-dry in a colander. When they are cool enough to handle, roughly break them into chunks.

Heat the oil in a large frying pan on a medium heat and add the cumin and mustard seeds. Fry until they start to pop. Add the onion and 1 teaspoon of salt and turn the heat down low to cook the onion really slowly. When the onion begins to soften – after about 5 minutes – add the garlic, ginger and green chilli, and cook until the onion is completely soft and caramelised (10–15 minutes in total).

Turn up the heat and add the curry powder, fresh tomatoes and a splash of water. Fry until the tomatoes begin to break down, then add the cooked potatoes, turmeric and a pinch of salt. Use a wooden spatula or spoon to break down some of the potatoes if needed, then add the coconut milk. Bring to a simmer, put a lid on the pan and cook on low for 5 minutes. Add the spinach and stir it through until it's wilted. Take the pan off the heat and add the lemon juice. Taste for seasoning. Serve topped with the coriander.

TOFU VEG BALTi

The classic balti is said to have been invented in the 1970s in Birmingham. 'Balti' refers to the thin metal dish the curry is cooked in, over a high flame. Balti curries are usually cooked quickly and fresh to order, almost like a stir-fry. As I imagine most of you won't have balti dishes lying around at home, I've recommended a wok for this recipe.

This dry curry works well served with rice, or noodles if you're feeling adventurous. You can sub out the suggested veg for whatever you have. It's best to use veg that can be stir-fried in the pan, but you can also throw in some pre-cooked veg such as cauliflower or broccoli.

Serves 4

260g firm tofu

5 tbsp veg oil

1 medium red onion, sliced into half-moons

5 large garlic cloves, grated or crushed

A thumb-sized piece of ginger, grated

2 green chillies, slit lengthways

10 fresh curry leaves (optional, leave out if you can't find fresh)

2 tbsp tomato purée

1 tsp sugar

3 medium tomatoes, roughly chopped

200g button mushrooms, quartered

2 tsp curry powder

1 tsp ground cumin

½ tbsp dried fenugreek leaves

A handful of green beans, topped and cut in half

A small handful of baby corn, slit lengthways and halved

1 tsp garam masala

Salt

A small bunch of coriander, roughly chopped (including stalks), to garnish

1 lime, quartered, to serve

Start by preparing the tofu. If it's in water, drain it and wrap it in kitchen paper or a clean tea towel. Gently press down on it to encourage any excess water out. Unwrap it and cut it into 1cm cubes.

Put a medium frying pan on a high heat and add 3 tablespoons of the oil. When it's smoking hot, carefully add the tofu cubes, one by one, so that each piece has a side face down in the oil. Add a generous pinch of salt. Leave to fry on one side for a couple of minutes until it has turned crispy and golden and then turn the pieces over, so they crisp up on another side. Repeat until all sides are crispy and golden. Put a piece of kitchen paper on a plate and transfer the cooked tofu onto the plate. Set to one side.

Put a large wok with the remaining 2 tablespoons of oil on a medium heat, and when it is hot add the onion and 1 teaspoon of salt. Turn the heat down low to cook the onion really slowly. When it starts to soften – after about 5 minutes – add the garlic, ginger, chillies and curry leaves, and cook until the onion is soft and caramelised and the smell of raw garlic has gone (10–15 minutes in total). Add the tomato purée and sugar and cook for 2 minutes until the purée has turned a darker shade of red.

Add the fresh tomatoes and mushrooms, followed by a sprinkling of salt, and fry until they begin to cook down. Add the curry powder, cumin and fenugreek leaves, and stir-fry for a couple of minutes. Then add the green beans, baby corn and garam masala, followed by 100ml water, and cook on a high heat until the veg has cooked through.

Finally, add the fried tofu and gently stir (you want to avoid breaking up the tofu). When the tofu is warmed through, take the pan off the heat. Taste for seasoning.

Garnish with coriander and serve with a wedge of lime.

PUMPKIN PASANDA

Pasandas are rich, meat-heavy curries which originated in the courts of the Mughal emperors. Pumpkins and squashes make for great meat replacements in curries like this, there's something regal and luxurious about a thick wedge of roasted seasonal squash swimming in a creamy curry sauce.

Serves 4

1 medium pumpkin or squash (choose from acorn, sweet dumpling, blue Hokkaido, kabocha or onion squashes or any sweet pumpkin variety)

3 tbsp veg oil, plus extra for roasting the pumpkin

2 cassia barks or cinnamon sticks

6 cardamom pods, crushed

2 medium-large white onions, finely diced

8 large garlic cloves, grated or crushed

A large thumb-sized piece of ginger, grated

2 tsp ground cumin

2 tsp ground coriander

1 tsp chilli powder

1 tsp ground turmeric

2 tsp sugar

8 tbsp ground almonds

800ml veg stock (page 32)

8 tbsp plain unsweetened soya yoghurt (I use Alpro)

A large bunch of coriander, roughly chopped (stalks included)

A handful of toasted flaked almonds, to garnish

Salt

Preheat the oven to 200°C. Wash the pumpkin or squash (scrub the skin with a scourer to remove any mud) and drizzle it with oil and a generous pinch of salt (fine sea salt works best). Use your hands to massage the oil and salt into the skin. Roast the squash or pumpkin in the oven for at least 40 minutes, or until the skin is golden and crispy and the flesh inside is really soft.

While the pumpkin or squash roasts, make the curry sauce. Heat the oil in a large casserole dish or frying pan on a medium heat and add the cassia barks or cinnamon sticks and cardamom pods. Fry until they are golden brown and aromatic. Add the onions and ½ teaspoon of salt and turn the heat down low to cook the onions really slowly. When the onions begin to soften – after about 5 minutes – add the garlic and ginger, and cook until the onions are completely soft and caramelised (10–15 minutes in total).

Add the rest of the ground spices, the sugar and a splash of water. Cook for a few minutes, then stir through the ground almonds. Toast the ground almonds in the spice mix for a few minutes, then add the veg stock. Turn the heat up to bring the pan to a simmer, then let it cook on low for 10 minutes until it has reduced.

When your pumpkin or squash is cooked, take it out of the oven and slice it into about six wedges. Use a spoon to scoop out the seeds and stringy flesh. Leave it to one side.

Add the yoghurt and three-quarters of the coriander to the curry sauce and taste for seasoning. Add the pumpkin or squash wedges and heat them through in the sauce. Take the pan off the heat and top with the flaked almonds and remaining coriander. Serve straight from the pan.

VEG DHANSAK

Dhansaks are lentil-based curries which originated among the Parsi community. They have become stalwarts of the British curry-house menu and are perfect examples of that addictive balance of sweet and sour flavours. At SpiceBox, we give our dhansak this sweet 'n' sour kick by using our homemade Date and Tamarind Chutney. As with all the curries in this book, the veg mix is up to you. One starchy and two or three fresh, sweet vegetables work well.

Serves 4

6 tbsp Date and Tamarind
    Chutney (page 215)
4 carrots, thinly sliced (skin on)
3 tbsp veg oil
2 tsp cumin seeds
1 medium red onion, sliced into
    half-moons
1 green chilli, slit lengthways
4 large garlic cloves, grated
    or crushed
A thumb-sized piece of ginger,
    grated
2 tbsp tomato purée
1 tsp sugar
3 medium tomatoes, roughly
    chopped
1 tsp ground cumin
1 tsp ground coriander
1 tsp curry powder
½ tsp hot chilli powder
100g split red lentils, rinsed
    in cold water
½ tsp ground turmeric
A handful of button mushrooms,
    quartered
A large handful of green beans,
    topped and cut in half
¼ cauliflower, cut into florets
    and roasted
Juice of ¼ lemon
Salt
A small bunch of coriander,
    roughly chopped (including
    stalks), to garnish

Start by making the Date and Tamarind Chutney (see page 215 for instructions).

Next, boil the carrots. Fill a saucepan with cold water and add 2 tablespoons of salt. Add the carrots and bring to the boil, then simmer until they're cooked. Drain and set aside until ready to use.

Now make the curry. Heat the oil in a large frying pan on a medium heat and add the cumin seeds. Fry until the seeds are golden and aromatic. Add the onion and 1 teaspoon of salt and turn the heat down low to cook the onion really slowly. When the onion begins to soften – after about 5 minutes – add the green chilli, garlic and ginger, and cook until the onion is completely soft and caramelised (10–15 minutes in total).

Turn up the heat and add the tomato purée and sugar. Cook for a couple of minutes until the purée has turned a darker shade of red. Add the fresh tomatoes and the rest of the spices, apart from the turmeric, along with a splash of water. Turn the heat down, cover the pan with a lid and cook for 5 minutes until the tomatoes begin to break down.

Turn the heat up to high and add the lentils and turmeric to the pan. Cover with 400ml water and put the lid back on. Bring to a simmer, then let it cook on low for 15 minutes, or until the lentils are soft and thick. Add the Date and Tamarind Chutney, followed by the mushrooms. Simmer until the mushrooms are soft, then add the rest of the veg. When all the veg are warmed through and the beans are cooked but still crunchy, take the pan off the heat and add the lemon juice. Taste for seasoning. Serve topped with fresh coriander.

MUM'S MUSHROOM & PEA CURRY

My love for India and Indian cooking was fuelled as much by my mum as it was by Auntie Dolly. Curry was her dinner party go-to and I often used to sit in the kitchen, watching her fry onions, garlic and ginger.

Mum was clearly influenced by Dolly when it came to Indian cooking, but she is also very much a member of the Madhur Jaffrey generation. When I became vegan, curries were the first dishes she turned to. She'd get the Madhur Jaffrey books out and flick through until we landed on a vegan curry or one that could be easily veganised. These recipes provided dishes that could unify our family of varied diets and tastes; carefully cooking vegetables with spices and aromatics can convince even the most ardent of meat-eaters that plant-based food can be complex and satisfying too.

This recipe is based on one of Mum's favourite Madhur Jaffrey recipes. She proudly calls it 'my mushroom and pea curry'. I've tweaked it slightly and made it vegan-friendly. This one's for you Mum!

Serves 4

3 tbsp veg oil
2 tsp cumin seeds
4 large garlic cloves, grated or crushed
A thumb-sized piece of ginger, grated
2 green chillies, thinly sliced
400g medium white mushrooms, quartered
1 tbsp tomato purée
1 tsp sugar
1½ tsp ground coriander
1½ tsp garam masala
250g frozen peas
400ml veg stock (page 32)
4 tbsp plain unsweetened soya yoghurt (I use Alpro)
A small bunch of coriander, roughly chopped (stalks included)
Salt
Crispy shallots (page 27)

Heat the oil in a large frying pan on a medium heat and add the cumin seeds. Fry until they're golden and aromatic and then add the garlic, ginger and chillies and a generous pinch of salt. Fry for a couple of minutes until the smell of raw garlic has gone and then add the mushrooms, tomato purée, sugar and another pinch of salt. Turn up the heat and stir-fry until the mushrooms begin to soften, then add the ground coriander and garam masala, followed by the frozen peas and veg stock. Simmer on a low heat for 5 minutes.

When the mushrooms are soft and the stock has reduced a little, take the pan off the heat and stir through the yoghurt and coriander. Taste for seasoning. Serve topped with crispy shallots.

TOFU & PEA CURRY

I have to admit, I have really missed paneer since going vegan. Muttar paneer was my go-to dish when I was travelling around India as a teenager – it's on pretty much every menu along the backpacker trail. There's something so comforting about rich, salty cubes of cheese in a creamy tomato sauce with the fresh pop of sweet peas.

I know many people are sceptical about tofu and that there will be raised eyebrows when I say tofu makes a great paneer replacement – but trust me on this.

Serves 4

300g good-quality extra-firm tofu
  (I use Tofoo, which can be found
  in most supermarkets)
6 tbsp veg oil
2 tsp cumin seeds
1 cassia bark or cinnamon stick
2 bay leaves
1 large red onion, sliced into
  half-moons
4 large garlic cloves, grated
  or crushed
A thumb-sized piece of ginger,
  grated
1 tsp chilli flakes
1 tsp ground coriander
1 tsp ground cumin
2 tbsp tomato purée
2 tsp sugar
1 tbsp red wine vinegar
2 medium tomatoes, roughly
  chopped
½ tsp ground turmeric
1 × 400ml tin of coconut milk
3 large handfuls of frozen peas
1 tsp garam masala
Juice of ½ lemon
Salt
A small bunch of coriander,
  roughly chopped (stalks
  included), to garnish

Start by preparing the tofu. If it's in water, drain it and wrap it in kitchen paper or a clean tea towel. Gently press down on it to encourage any excess water out. Unwrap it and cut it into 1cm cubes.

Put a large frying pan on a high heat and add 3 tablespoons of the oil. When it's smoking hot, carefully add the tofu cubes, one by one, so that each piece has a side face down in the oil. Sprinkle generously with salt. Leave to fry on one side for a couple of minutes until it has turned crispy and golden and then turn the pieces over, repeating until all sides are golden. Drain the tofu on a piece of kitchen paper on a plate and set to one side.

Now make the curry sauce. Heat the remaining 3 tablespoons of oil in a large frying pan on a medium heat and add the cumin seeds, cassia bark or cinnamon stick and bay leaves. Fry until the seeds are golden and aromatic. Add the onion and 1 teaspoon of salt and turn the heat down low to cook the onion really slowly. When the onion begins to soften, add the garlic and ginger, and cook until the onion is completely soft and caramelised (10–15 minutes in total).

Add the chilli flakes, ground coriander and ground cumin, along with a splash of water. Stir-fry for a couple of minutes, then add the tomato purée and sugar. Cook for 2 minutes until the purée has turned a darker shade of red, then add the vinegar followed by the fresh tomatoes, turmeric and another splash of water if needed. Turn the heat up to bring the pan to a simmer, cover with a lid and leave to cook on a low heat for 5 minutes until the tomatoes are soft. Take the lid off and add the coconut milk. When it's simmering, add the tofu and peas followed by the garam masala. Simmer until the peas are cooked through. Take the pan off the heat and stir through the lemon juice. Taste for seasoning. Serve topped with the chopped coriander. This curry tastes delicious with the Spring Radish Pickle on page 231.

JACKFRUiT JALFREZi

This is the dish that made SpiceBox! It has been on the menu since day one, when jackfruit was still a relatively unknown ingredient in the UK. The only place I could buy tinned young jackfruit was Banglatown cash and carry off Brick Lane. The busier SpiceBox became, the lower their stock levels ran. Every week, I'd make a pilgrimage to Banglatown in my van and buy up every tin they had in stock but eventually I outgrew their supply cycle. This meant a mad dash around London on my bike, scouring Asian supermarkets for that familiar yellow and green tin, a wave of relief washing over me when I spied it on the shelf among the cans of coconut milk and mango.

Fortunately, the UK has moved on since then and young jackfruit can now be found in most supermarkets (oh to think how easy life would have been …). It can also be ordered online. Avoid buying the sweet yellow jackfruit as you'll end up with a dessert rather than a curry.

Jalfrezis are spicy and this recipe doesn't hold back on the heat. Don't be put off by the amount of chilli – it's important to layer the different chillies on top of each other, as they all bring a unique flavour. If your chilli threshold is low, leave out the chilli powder and replace the chopped green chillies with coriander for garnish.

Serves 4

For the jackfruit marinade
2 × 560g tins of young jackfruit,
    drained and rinsed
3 tbsp veg oil
1 tsp ground cumin
1 tsp smoked paprika
1 tsp chilli powder
1 tsp ground coriander
½ tsp ground turmeric
2 tbsp light or dark soy sauce
2 tsp sugar

Ingredients cont. page 76

First prepare the jackfruit. Place it in a large bowl and use your hands to tear it up into small pieces. It should resemble pulled pork. Add the rest of the marinade ingredients and use your hands to massage the marinade into the jackfruit. Set to one side for at least 15 minutes and up to 12 hours. When you are ready to cook, preheat the oven to 220°C.

Roast the jackfruit in the oven for 20 minutes, or until it's crispy around the edges. You will need to stir it halfway through roasting.

Recipe cont. page 76

For the curry sauce

4 tbsp veg oil

1 bay leaf

1 dried red chilli, ripped into
    quarters

2 medium white onions, sliced
    into half-moons

4 large garlic cloves, grated
    or crushed

A thumb-sized piece of ginger,
    grated

2 green chillies, thinly sliced

2 green peppers, thinly sliced

2 tbsp tomato purée

2 tsp sugar

1 tsp chilli powder

1 tsp smoked paprika

1 tsp ground cumin

1 tsp ground coriander

½ tsp ground turmeric

500g passata or chopped
    tomatoes

2 tbsp light or dark soy sauce

1 tbsp vinegar

Salt

Now make the curry sauce. Heat the oil in a large frying pan on a medium heat, add the bay leaf and dried red chilli, and fry until golden. Add the onions and 1 teaspoon of salt and turn the heat down low to cook the onion really slowly. When the onions begin to soften – after about 5 minutes – add the garlic, ginger, 1 green chilli and the green peppers, and cook until the onions are completely soft and caramelised and the peppers are soft (10–15 minutes in total).

Add the tomato purée, sugar and rest of the ground spices. You may need to add a splash of water to stop them burning. Stir-fry for a couple of minutes until the purée has turned a darker shade of red.

Turn up the heat and add the passata, followed by the soy sauce, vinegar, roasted jackfruit and a splash of water. Simmer on a low heat for 15 minutes. Taste for seasoning. Serve topped with the remaining sliced green chilli.

ROGAN SQUASH

There's more to squash than butternut. Make a trip to your local farmers' market between autumn and spring for a variety of different squashes of all sizes, shapes and colours – from the bulbous turban, to the beautiful duck egg blue Hokkaido, the ridged racing green acorn and neat round red onion. Each has its own distinct texture and flavour, and I encourage you to buy a few different small ones to try out. If you can't get to a farmers' market, butternut squashes are available all year round and work well.

Serves 4

1 extra-large squash (or 2 medium ones), deseeded and cut into 1.5cm chunks (leave the skin on)
4 tbsp veg oil, plus extra for roasting the veg
6 medium tomatoes, cut in half
1 tsp coriander seeds
2 black peppercorns
2 cardamom pods
1 tsp fennel seeds
2 bay leaves
1 cassia bark or cinnamon stick
2 cloves
2 dried red chillies (preferably Kashmiri), ripped into quarters
1 large red onion, sliced
4 large garlic cloves, crushed
A thumb-sized piece of ginger, grated
2 tbsp tomato purée
1 tsp sugar
1 tsp smoked paprika
1 tsp ground cumin
½ tsp ground turmeric
½ tsp ground cinnamon
300ml gravy made from granules (I use Bisto)
4 tbsp plain unsweetened soya yoghurt (I use Alpro)
Juice of ½ lemon
Salt
A small bunch of coriander, roughly chopped, to garnish

Preheat the oven to 200°C.

Put the squash on a baking tray (or two if needed) and drizzle with oil and a generous pinch of salt. Roast in the oven for 30–40 minutes until the skin is golden and the flesh is soft – you want it to still have some bite at this stage.

Place the tomatoes, cut-side up, on a baking tray, drizzle with oil and sprinkle over a pinch of salt. Roast in the oven for 20 minutes or until soft and caramelised.

While your veg is roasting, make the sauce. Put the coriander seeds, peppercorns and cardamom pods in a pestle and mortar and lightly crush. If you don't have a pestle and mortar, crush them slightly with a sharp knife.

Heat the oil in a large frying pan on a medium heat and add the spice mix along with the fennel seeds, bay leaves, cassia bark or cinnamon stick and cloves. When they are golden and aromatic, add the dried chillies, onion and 1 teaspoon of salt and turn the heat down low to cook the onion really slowly. When the onion begins to soften – after about 5 minutes – add the garlic and ginger, and cook until the onion is completely soft and caramelised (10–15 minutes in total).

Turn up the heat and add the tomato purée, sugar and rest of the ground spices. You may need to add a splash of water to stop the spices burning. Stir-fry for a couple of minutes until the purée has turned a darker shade of red. Add the roasted squash and tomatoes and stir so they're well coated with the spice mix. Pour in the gravy, turn down the heat and simmer for 10 minutes until the sauce has reduced slightly and the squash is soft.

Take the pan off the heat and stir through the yoghurt and lemon juice. Taste for seasoning. Serve topped with the coriander.

CHANA MASALA

This is my favourite curry on the SpiceBox menu. It's simple in method yet complex in flavour – sweet slow-cooked onions, base notes of cinnamon, a slow subtle build of heat from the dried chillies and black pepper, and sweet and sour top notes from the passata. This is plant-based Indian food at its finest.

Serves 4

For the spiced chickpeas
2 × 400g tins of chickpeas, drained and rinsed
1 tsp ground black pepper
1 tsp ground cinnamon
1 tsp fine sea salt

For the curry sauce
150ml veg oil
1 large cassia bark or cinnamon stick
2 tsp cumin seeds
A small bunch of coriander, roughly chopped (stalks included), plus a few picked leaves to garnish
2 dried red chillies, ripped into quarters
2½ medium red onions, sliced into half-moons (save the half to garnish)
4 large garlic cloves, grated or crushed
A thumb-sized piece of ginger, grated
2 tbsp tomato purée
1 tsp sugar
400g passata or chopped tomatoes
1 tsp garam masala
Salt

First prepare the chickpeas. Put them in a large bowl with the pepper, cinnamon and salt. Stir well until all the chickpeas are coated and set aside while you make the curry sauce.

Heat the oil in a large frying pan on a medium heat and add the cassia bark or cinnamon stick and cumin seeds. Fry until the seeds are golden and aromatic. Carefully add the fresh coriander – watch out for spitting oil. When it has turned a darker shade of green and smells amazing, add the dried chillies, onions and 1 teaspoon of salt. Turn the heat down low to cook the onions really slowly. When the onions begin to soften – after about 5 minutes – add the garlic and ginger, and cook until the onions are completely soft and caramelised (at least 15 minutes). It is really important that you cook the onions down for as long as possible in this dish – its success lies in the sweetness of the cooked onions.

Add the tomato purée and sugar and stir-fry for 2 minutes until the purée has turned a darker shade of red. Turn up the heat and add the chickpeas. Fry the chickpeas for a couple of minutes, then add the passata or chopped tomatoes and garam masala. Simmer for 15 minutes until the sauce has reduced a little and the chickpeas are buttery soft. Taste for seasoning. Serve topped with the remaining sliced red onion and the picked coriander leaves.

AUBERGiNE MALAi

Malai is a dish originally from West Bengal and traditionally made with prawns simmered in a creamy coconut sauce. I've replaced the prawns with soft buttery aubergines. I usually cook aubergines with tomato but there's something luxurious about caramelised aubergines melting into a thick creamy sauce. The lime and kaffir lime leaves help cut through the richness.

Serves 4

For the aubergines
4 medium aubergines, cut into
  1.5cm cubes
1 tbsp veg oil
1 tsp ground turmeric
Salt

For the curry sauce
1 medium white onion, roughly
  chopped
4 large garlic cloves, roughly
  chopped
A thumb-sized piece of ginger,
  roughly chopped
2 green chillies, roughly chopped
4 tbsp desiccated coconut
150ml veg oil
1 cassia bark or cinnamon stick
4 cardamom pods, crushed
2 cloves
3 kaffir lime leaves
1 tsp sugar
1 tsp chilli powder
1 tsp garam masala
1 × 400ml tin of coconut milk
Zest and juice of 1 lime
Coconut flakes, toasted
  (page 38), to garnish
A small bunch of coriander,
  roughly chopped, to garnish

First prepare the aubergines. Place the pieces in a large bowl and add the oil, 2 teaspoons of salt and the turmeric and mix well. Set to one side for at least 15 minutes.

Now make your onion paste. Put the onion, garlic, ginger, green chillies and desiccated coconut in a small blender and blitz until a paste is formed. Add a splash of water if needed to get it going.

Heat the oil in a large frying pan or wok on a medium heat. Add the cassia bark or cinnamon stick, cardamom pods and cloves, and fry until they're golden and aromatic. Add the kaffir lime leaves, followed by the onion paste and a pinch of salt. Turn the heat down low to cook the onion slowly, until the smell of raw garlic and onion has gone. This will take around 10 minutes.

Turn up the heat and add the aubergines. Fry until they begin to soften and caramelise, then add the sugar, chilli powder and garam masala. Fry for a further 10 minutes until the aubergines begin to release their flavoured oil back into the pan. Be patient – it will happen and it's the secret to super-sweet, buttery aubergines. Add the coconut milk, bring to a simmer, then let it cook on a low heat for 5 minutes.

Take the pan off the heat and add the lime zest and juice. Taste for seasoning. Serve topped with the toasted coconut flakes and chopped coriander.

WiLD MUSHROOM PALAK 'GOSHT'

Palak gosht is a Punjabi dish traditionally made with slow-cooked mutton (the *gosht*) and spinach (*palak*). I find mushrooms make a really great meat replacement in dishes like this – they're meaty in texture and taste and are also great at absorbing flavours. Most supermarkets now sell mixes of wild and exotic mushrooms – it's up to you which mushrooms you go for but make sure you use mushrooms with different textures and sizes.

Serves 4

4 tbsp veg oil
1 cassia bark or cinnamon stick
3 cardamom pods, crushed
1 medium red onion, finely diced
6 large garlic cloves, grated
   or crushed
A thumb-sized piece of ginger,
   grated
2 green chillies, thinly sliced
400g mixed wild mushrooms,
   roughly sliced
1 tbsp tomato purée
1 tsp sugar
2 medium tomatoes, finely diced
1 tsp ground cumin
1 tsp ground coriander
½ tsp ground turmeric
1 tbsp coconut oil
550g spinach, finely shredded
8 tbsp plain unsweetened soya
   yoghurt (I use Alpro)
1 tsp garam masala
Juice of ½ lemon
Salt

Heat the oil in a large saucepan on a medium heat and add the cassia bark or cinnamon stick and the cardamom pods. Fry until golden and aromatic. Add the onion and 1 teaspoon of salt and turn the heat down low to cook the onion really slowly. When the onion begins to soften – after about 5 minutes – add the garlic, ginger and chillies, and cook until the onion is completely soft and caramelised (10–15 minutes in total).

Turn up the heat and add the mushrooms, along with a pinch of salt. Fry until they begin to soften, then add the tomato purée and sugar. Fry for a few minutes, then add the fresh tomatoes, followed by the ground spices (apart from the garam masala). Cook until the tomatoes begin to break down, then add the coconut oil and spinach. Cover the pan with a lid and cook for 5 minutes until the spinach has completely wilted down. Finish by stirring through the yoghurt, garam masala and lemon juice. Taste for seasoning.

TOFU SAAG 'PANEER'

Saag paneer comes in many forms – it can be a rich and saucy dish made with a creamy blended spinach sauce, a dry dish made with tinned or frozen spinach, or, as I like best, a light fresh curry made with big leaves of spinach, a squeeze of lemon and a good kick of fenugreek.

I've used tofu to replace paneer here and it works perfectly. This light, zesty curry is ideal to enjoy in warm weather or when you're feeling like a light nutritious meal. I prefer to keep the spinach leaves whole, rather than blend them so don't expect loads of sauce. This is great served with fresh roti or puri (page 146 and page 143).

Serves 4

300g extra-firm tofu (I use Tofoo, which can be found in most supermarkets)
6 tbsp veg oil
4 large garlic cloves, roughly chopped
A thumb-sized piece of ginger, roughly chopped
2 tsp cumin seeds
1 tsp fenugreek seeds
1 green chilli, thinly sliced
2 medium tomatoes, roughly chopped
½ tsp ground turmeric
700g large-leaf spinach, roughly shredded
½ tsp ground black pepper
Whole nutmeg, to season
Juice of ½ lemon
Salt

Start by preparing the tofu. If it's in water, drain it and wrap it in kitchen paper or a clean tea towel. Gently press down on it to encourage any excess water out. Unwrap it and cut it into rectangles (roughly 1 × 1.5cm).

Put a large frying pan on a high heat and add 3 tablespoons of oil. When it's smoking hot, carefully add the tofu cubes, one by one, so that each piece has a side face down in the oil. Sprinkle generously with salt. Leave to fry on one side for a couple of minutes until it has turned crispy and golden and then turn the pieces over, so they crisp up on another side. Repeat until all sides are crispy and golden. Drain the tofu on a piece of kitchen paper and set to one side.

Place the garlic and ginger in a small blender with a splash of water and blitz until you have a smooth paste. Set to one side.

Heat the remaining 3 tablespoons of oil in a large frying pan on a medium heat and add the cumin seeds. Fry until they are golden and aromatic, then add the fenugreek seeds and fry for a few seconds, before adding the garlic and ginger paste, followed by a generous pinch of salt. Cook for a couple of minutes and then add the green chilli, fresh tomatoes, turmeric and 100ml water. Simmer until the tomatoes begin to break down, then add the spinach – this will need to be done in stages, but don't worry, the spinach will wilt quickly.

When all the spinach has reduced down, add the tofu and a generous pinch of salt. Add the black pepper and grate over the nutmeg (around 7 grates should be enough to flavour the dish without overpowering it).

Take the pan off the heat and stir though the lemon juice. Taste for seasoning.

JACKFRUIT VINDALOO

Vindaloos are famous for their fiery spice, but it's not the heat that draws me to them – it's the kick of sourness from the tamarind and vinegar. I add a touch of sugar to balance this out slightly and, as explained on page 30, this is a really helpful trick when cooking any tomato-based curry. Sweet (from the sugar) and sour (from the vinegar) really help bring out the flavour of tomatoes.

Jackfruit works really well in this recipe as it absorbs the flavours of the punchy sauce and gives a texture similar to slow-cooked meat.

Serves 4

For the jackfruit marinade
2 × 560g tins of young green
    jackfruit, drained and rinsed
1 tbsp veg oil
1 tsp fine sea salt
1 tsp sugar
2 tsp smoked paprika
1 tsp ground black pepper

For the curry sauce
150ml veg oil
1 cassia bark or cinnamon stick
2 cloves
3 cardamom pods, crushed
1 tsp cumin seeds
1 tsp brown mustard seeds
2 tsp chilli flakes
2 medium red onions, sliced
    into half-moons
6 large garlic cloves, grated
    or crushed
A thumb-sized piece of ginger,
    grated
2 green chillies, thinly sliced
1 tsp ground cumin
1 tsp ground coriander
1 tsp ground black pepper
2 tsp chilli powder
½ tsp ground turmeric
2 tbsp tomato purée
1 tbsp sugar
3 medium tomatoes, finely diced
1 tbsp tamarind paste
3 tbsp red wine vinegar
1 tsp garam masala
1 × 400g tin of chopped tomatoes
Salt
A small bunch of coriander,
    roughly chopped (stalks
    included), to garnish

First prepare the jackfruit. Place it in a large bowl and use your hands to tear it up into small pieces. It should resemble pulled pork. Add the rest of the marinade ingredients and use your hands to massage the marinade into the jackfruit. Set to one side while you make the curry sauce.

Heat the oil in a large frying pan on a medium heat and add the cassia bark or cinnamon stick, cloves, cardamom pods, cumin and mustard seeds. Fry until golden and aromatic. Add the chilli flakes, followed by the onions and 1 teaspoon of salt and turn the heat down low to cook the onions slowly. When the onions begin to soften – after about 5 minutes – add the garlic, ginger and green chillies, and cook until the onions are completely soft and caramelised (10–15 minutes in total).

Turn the heat up to medium and add the jackfruit and ground spices (apart from the garam masala). Fry for 5 minutes until the jackfruit begins to caramelise and crisp around the edges. Add the tomato purée and sugar and fry for a couple of minutes, before adding the fresh tomatoes. When the tomatoes begin to break down, add the tamarind paste, vinegar and garam masala, and cook for a few minutes.

Add the chopped tomatoes, fill the empty tin with water and rinse it out into the pan. Turn the heat down low and simmer for 20 minutes until the sauce has reduced a little and the flavours have intensified. Taste for seasoning. When it's ready, take the pan off the heat and stir through the chopped coriander.

CURRY-CRUSTED TANDOORi BROCCOLi

Although this isn't technically a curry (when baked, the sauce forms a crust around the broccoli), it is certainly worthy of sitting centre-stage at the dinner table. Serve this with roti (page 146) and a saucy side, such as Tarka Dhal (page 108).

Serves 4

For the broccoli
1 tsp ground turmeric
2 tsp fine sea salt
1 large or 2 medium heads
   of broccoli

For the curry sauce/crust
150g cashew nuts
3 tbsp veg oil
1 medium white onion, roughly
   chopped
4 large garlic cloves, roughly
   chopped
A thumb-sized piece of ginger,
   roughly chopped
4 medium tomatoes, roughly
   chopped
1 tsp sugar
1 tbsp dried fenugreek leaves
2 tsp ground cumin
1 tsp ground coriander
½ tsp ground turmeric
1 tbsp curry powder
Salt
A handful of flaked almonds,
   toasted, to garnish
A small bunch of coriander,
   roughly chopped (stalks
   included), to garnish
A pinch of chilli flakes (optional
   if you like chilli), to garnish

Cover the cashews with cold water and leave them to soak for at least 2 hours.

Preheat the oven to 200°C.

First prepare the broccoli. Put a large saucepan of water for each head of broccoli on to boil, and add the turmeric and salt (if using two pans, divide between them). Place the broccoli head(s) upside down in the boiling water, cover with a lid and boil for 2 minutes until the broccoli is starting to soften. Drain and set aside to cool. When the broccoli is cool enough to handle, slice the head(s) lengthways down the middle and set aside until ready to use.

Heat the oil in a large frying pan and add the onion and 1 teaspoon of salt. Turn the heat down low to cook the onion really slowly. When it begins to soften – after about 5 minutes – add the garlic and ginger, and cook until the onion is completely soft and caramelised (10–15 minutes in total). Add the fresh tomatoes, sugar and fenugreek leaves, and fry for a couple of minutes, then add the rest of the spices, along with a splash of water if needed. Cook until the tomatoes begin to break down.

Transfer the cooked onion and tomato mix to a blender with the drained cashews, a large pinch of salt and 300ml water. Blitz until a smooth creamy sauce is formed.

Place the broccoli heads flat-side down in a large ovenproof casserole dish with a lid and pour over the sauce. Put on the lid and bake in the oven for 30 minutes, until they are cooked through and have formed a golden crust. If needed, you can always pop them under a hot grill for a minute to turn the tops golden brown.

Serve straight from the dish, topped with the flaked almonds, chopped coriander and chilli flakes (if using). This is great with Mango and Apricot Chutney (page 222) and Raita (page 232).

DOM'S HARiYALi

Dom joined SpiceBox during our pop-up at the Hornbeam Café in Walthamstow in 2018. He started as a kitchen porter but soon began working the odd shift as a chef. Dom has grown to become one of our best chefs in the curry house and so, around a year after he joined us, we handed over our monthly special to him. His creation was this hariyali. It was the first hariyali I'd tried and I *loved* it – the herbs and peas give an amazing freshness and the coriander seeds top everything off with a fragrant flowery note.

Thanks Dom for all your hard work with us, and thank you for letting me use your recipe!

Serves 4

For the paste
3 large bunches of coriander (stalks included)
A large bunch of mint (leaves only)
2 green chillies
Juice of 1 lime
½ tsp fine sea salt

For the curry sauce
3 medium potatoes
3 tbsp veg oil
1 tsp coriander seeds, lightly crushed
1 tsp cumin seeds
½ tsp fenugreek seeds
1 medium red onion, finely diced
6 large garlic cloves, grated or crushed
A large thumb-sized piece of ginger, grated
½ tsp ground turmeric
1 tsp garam masala
1 tsp sugar
300g frozen peas
4 tbsp plain unsweetened soya yoghurt (I use Alpro)
Juice of ¼ lemon
Salt

First prepare the potatoes. Fill a large saucepan with water and add 2 tablespoons of salt. Add the potatoes whole (don't peel them!) and bring to the boil. Cook until they are nice and soft – this will take at least 40 minutes from cold but will depend on size and variety. Once the skin begins to crack, test if they're ready by poking them with a fork – it should slide very easily into the potatoes. Drain and leave to steam-dry in a colander. When they are cool enough to handle, roughly dice them.

While the potatoes are cooking, make the paste. Place everything in a blender with 400ml water and blitz until smooth.

Now make the curry sauce. Heat the oil in a large frying pan on a medium heat and add the coriander, cumin and fenugreek seeds. Fry until the seeds are golden and aromatic. Add the onion and 1 teaspoon of salt and turn the heat down low to cook the onion really slowly. When the onion begins to soften – after about 5 minutes – add the garlic and ginger, and cook until the onion is completely soft and caramelised (10–15 minutes in total).

Add the turmeric, garam masala and sugar, and fry for a couple of minutes. Then add the herby paste, frozen peas and potatoes, and simmer until the peas are cooked through. Take the pan off the heat and stir through the yoghurt and lemon juice. Taste for seasoning.

PUNJABi CHOLE

I ate my first chole in Delhi at a tiny roadside café famous for its rich, dark chickpea curry. I will never forget the flavours – multiple layers of earthy spices and buttery soft chickpeas that melt in the mouth. A traditional chole recipe calls for the chickpeas to be cooked from dry – slowly simmered in tea-infused water. However, without a pressure cooker, it's difficult to achieve that melt-in-your-mouth chickpea texture and you'll probably max out your energy bill trying to get there. I've therefore used tinned chickpeas in this recipe.

If you can't find chole masala powder, you can replace it with 1 teaspoon of ground cumin, ½ teaspoon of ground cinnamon, ½ teaspoon of ground black pepper, ½ teaspoon of chilli powder and ½ teaspoon of grated nutmeg.

Serves 4

For the tea-steeped chickpeas
2 × 400g tins of cooked
  chickpeas, drained and rinsed
2 black teabags
2 black cardamom pods, lightly
  crushed
1 tsp fine sea salt

For the curry sauce
150ml veg oil
2 bay leaves
1 black cardamom pod, lightly
  crushed
2 tsp cumin seeds
1½ large red onions, sliced
  (save the half to garnish)
A large thumb-sized piece of
  ginger, grated, plus a smaller
  piece, cut into thin matchsticks
2 green chillies, slit lengthways
1 tbsp chole masala powder
  (see introduction)
2 tsp ground coriander
2 tsp garam masala
1 tsp chilli powder
2 tbsp tomato purée
1 tsp sugar
Salt

First prepare the chickpeas. Put them in a saucepan and cover with 500ml cold water. Add the teabags, cardamom pods and salt, and bring to the boil. Turn the heat down and simmer for 5 minutes, then take them off the heat and leave to sit in the tea water for at least 10 minutes.

While your chickpeas are infusing in the tea water, make the curry sauce. Heat the oil in a large frying pan on a medium heat and add the bay leaves, cardamom pod and cumin seeds. Fry until the seeds are golden and aromatic. Add the onion and 1 teaspoon of salt and turn the heat down low to cook the onion really slowly. When the onion begins to soften – after about 5 minutes – add the grated ginger and green chillies, and cook until the onion is completely soft and caramelised (10–15 minutes in total).

Add the ground spices and fry for a minute or so. You can add a splash of water if they start to stick. Then add the tomato purée and sugar, and fry for 2 minutes until the purée has turned a darker shade of red.

Remove the teabags and cardamom pods from the chickpeas and drain the liquid into a bowl – you need to keep the cooking liquid.

Turn up the heat under the frying pan and add the chickpeas, stirring so they're well coated with the spice mix. Add 400ml of the chickpea cooking liquid and simmer on a low heat for 5 minutes until the chickpeas are super-soft and buttery and the sauce has reduced slightly. Taste for seasoning. Serve topped with the remaining red onion and the matchsticks of ginger.

SHROOM 'KEEMA'

Keema is a dry mince-based dish often made with ground mutton and peas. You may be familiar with it from seeing keema naans on curry-house menus – Indian flatbreads stuffed with spiced minced meat. This is my vegan keema and people go crazy for it at SpiceBox.

This recipe is super-versatile and can be used as mince in a shepherd's pie, lasagne or bolognese, to give an extra spicy kick. You can buy dried soya mince (sometimes known as textured vegetable protein or TVP) online or from most health food shops.

Serves 4

For the rehydrated soya mince
80g dried soya mince
550ml boiling water
1 black teabag
2 tsp Marmite
1 tsp ground black pepper
2 tbsp light or dark soy sauce

For the curry
1 medium white onion, roughly
    chopped
6 large garlic cloves, roughly
    chopped
A thumb-sized piece of ginger,
    roughly chopped
3 tbsp veg oil
1 tsp ground cumin
½ tsp ground coriander
½ tsp chilli powder
½ tsp ground black pepper
1 tbsp tomato purée
1 tsp sugar
150g button mushrooms, very
    finely diced
150g walnuts, roasted and blitzed
    into fine pieces
1 tsp garam masala
Whole nutmeg, to season
1 tbsp light or dark soy sauce
160g frozen peas
Salt
1 green chilli, thinly sliced,
    to garnish

Start by preparing the soya mince. Put the dried mince in a medium saucepan and cover with the boiling water. Add the teabag, Marmite, black pepper and soy sauce. Leave the mince to rehydrate for a minimum of 10 minutes.

While the mince is rehydrating, put the onion, garlic and ginger in a blender with 1 teaspoon of salt and blitz until a smooth paste is formed. Heat the oil in a large frying pan on a medium heat and add the onion paste. Turn the heat down low and fry until the paste is cooked through – this will take around 10 minutes.

When the paste is cooked, add the cumin, coriander, chilli powder and black pepper, and fry for a couple of minutes. Stir through the tomato purée and sugar, and fry for 5 minutes until the purée has turned a darker shade of red. Add the mushrooms and fry until they begin to cook down. Add the blitzed walnuts and stir, before adding the soaked mince and any water that is left in the pan – make sure you remove the teabag.

Turn up the heat and when the mixture begins to bubble, add the garam masala and grate over the nutmeg (about 7 grates should be enough). Add the soy sauce, followed by the frozen peas and stir well. Simmer until the peas are cooked through. Taste for seasoning.

Serve topped with the sliced green chilli.

'BUTTER' CAULiFLOWER

This is a plant-based spin on butter chicken – a decadent creamy curry that traditionally contains, you guessed it, *a lot* of butter! I've used coconut oil instead of butter, which gives the same richness, and cashew cream instead of cream, which adds an amazing nutty flavour as well as a creamy texture.

Shortly after we opened the curry house, we did a collaboration with my friend Clare, aka 'The Little London Vegan'. I asked her to pick a dish she'd love to see on our menu and she immediately chose 'Butter Chicken'. Clare told me how she used to always order it and would love to try it 'veganised'. And so I got to work on putting a SpiceBox spin on this curry-house classic.

If you're in the mood for a full-on curry night experience, this dish should be on your menu. *Pictured overleaf*

Serves 4

For the cauliflower marinade

300g plain unsweetened soya
  yoghurt (I use Alpro)
2 tsp smoked paprika
1 tsp ground cumin
1 tsp ground coriander
½ tsp fine sea salt
4 large garlic cloves, grated
  or crushed
A thumb-sized piece of ginger,
  peeled and grated
Juice of ½ lemon
2 medium cauliflowers, cut into
  florets (keep the inner leaves)

For the curry sauce

150g cashew nuts
4 tbsp veg oil, plus extra for
  roasting the veg
1 large white onion, roughly
  chopped
4 large garlic cloves, roughly
  chopped
A thumb-sized piece of ginger,
  roughly chopped
1 green chilli, roughly chopped
1 tbsp coconut oil
1 tsp garam masala
½ tsp chilli powder
1 tsp smoked paprika
1 tsp curry powder
250g passata or chopped
  tomatoes
2 tbsp red wine vinegar
1 tsp sugar
Juice of ½ lemon
Salt
A small bunch of coriander,
  roughly chopped, to garnish
A swirl of oat or soya cream,
  to garnish

Start by making the marinade for the cauliflower – well in advance of when you want to cook. Place all the marinade ingredients in a bowl and mix well. Add the cauliflower florets and soft inner leaves and coat evenly in the marinade. Leave for at least 30 minutes and up to 12 hours covered in the fridge.

Next, cover the cashews with cold water and leave them to soak for at least 2 hours.

When you are ready to cook, preheat your oven to 220°C.

Place the marinated cauliflower florets in a well-oiled roasting tin and roast in the oven for 30 minutes or until soft and golden. Halfway through, give the cauliflower a stir and add the leaves.

Now make the curry sauce. Heat the oil in a large frying pan over a medium heat and add the onion and 1 teaspoon of salt. Turn the heat down low to cook the onion really slowly. When the onion begins to soften – after about 5 minutes – add the garlic, ginger and green chilli, and cook until the onion is completely soft and caramelised (10–15 minutes in total).

Add the coconut oil and the rest of the spices and cook for a few minutes. Stir through the passata or chopped tomatoes, vinegar and sugar. Take the pan off the heat and transfer the sauce to a blender. Add the drained cashews and 500ml cold water, and blitz until a smooth creamy sauce is formed.

Pour the sauce back into the frying pan and add the roasted cauliflower and leaves. Bring the curry up to the boil, then simmer on a low heat for 5 minutes. Take the pan off the heat and add the lemon juice. Taste for seasoning.

Serve topped with the coriander and a swirl of oat cream.

PEANUT CURRY WiTH SWEET POTATO & SPiNACH

I first encountered peanut curry while staying on a family-run spice plantation on the Konkan coast, on the western side of India. It struck a real chord with me as it was the first time I'd eaten an Indian curry with this sort of flavour profile – creamy coconut milk, sweet and sour tamarind and nutty richness from the peanuts. To me, it was reminiscent of Southeast Asian flavours. The lime and spring onion garnish add an essential fresh kick to the dish and another nod to Southeast Asia, although you do often find spring onion used as a garnish on many tables in South India too.

Peanut curry is usually found in Western Indian cuisine and is often made during fasting. This recipe, however, is based on a Hyderabadi wedding dish called 'Salan'. A salan is a peanut spice paste usually made with freshly ground peanuts. I've sped things up here with peanut butter; it adds an amazing richness and thickness to the sauce without the need for lengthy simmering. *Pictured on previous page*

Serves 4

For the salan (peanut spice paste)
1 tbsp coriander seeds
2 tsp cumin seeds
1 tbsp sesame seeds
2 tbsp desiccated coconut
4 tbsp crunchy peanut butter
(ideally made from 100%
peanuts)
6 garlic cloves
A thumb-sized piece of ginger,
roughly chopped

For the curry sauce
2 tbsp veg oil
2 tsp brown mustard seeds
1 tsp fenugreek seeds
10 fresh curry leaves (optional,
leave out if you can't find fresh)
1 large white onion, sliced into
half-moons
1 green chilli, finely chopped
2 tbsp tomato purée
1 tsp sugar
4 medium tomatoes, roughly
chopped
1 tsp chilli powder
1 tsp ground turmeric
1 × 400ml tin of coconut milk
2 tbsp tamarind paste
1 large sweet potato, cut into
1.5cm chunks (skin on)
250g green beans, topped and
cut in half
3 large handfuls of spinach,
roughly shredded
Salt
A small bunch of spring onions,
thinly sliced, to garnish
A handful of roasted peanuts,
chopped, to garnish
1 lime, quartered, to garnish

Start by making the peanut spice paste. Dry-roast the coriander seeds, cumin seeds, sesame seeds and coconut in a frying pan on a medium heat until they've turned golden and aromatic. Tip into a small blender or food processor, along with the other paste ingredients and 100ml water. Blend until smooth and set the paste to one side.

Now make the sauce. Heat the oil in a large frying pan or saucepan on a medium heat and add the mustard seeds. Fry until they begin to pop, then add the fenugreek seeds and curry leaves. When these begin to turn golden and release their distinctive aroma, add the onion and 1 teaspoon of salt and cook slowly on a low heat until the onion is completely soft and caramelised (10–15 minutes). Add the green chilli, tomato purée, sugar and peanut spice paste, and fry for at least 5 minutes – the spice paste must be cooked all the way through.

When the mixture is cooked and smelling delicious, add the fresh tomatoes, chilli powder and turmeric. Turn the heat up to medium and cook until the tomatoes start to dissolve into the sauce. Add the coconut milk, tamarind paste and 150ml water, and give everything a good stir.

Add the sweet potato to the sauce. If you think it needs more water, add some. The sauce should be thick but there needs to be enough liquid for the sweet potato to cook. Cover the pan with a lid and simmer for 15–20 minutes until the sweet potato is cooked through.

Add the beans and simmer for around 3 minutes until they're cooked through but still crunchy, then stir through the spinach until wilted. Taste for seasoning. There should be a good balance between the sweetness of the coconut and tomatoes, the sourness of the tamarind, and the salt. If you think it needs any more, add salt, sugar or tamarind accordingly.

Serve topped with the sliced spring onions, chopped peanuts and lime wedges on the side.

ROASTED TOMATO & AUBERGINE CURRY

Roasting the aubergine, tomatoes and garlic adds a rich, smoky flavour to this curry. When we served it at the curry house as a special one month, our guests begged us to keep it on the menu. If you're an aubergine lover, this one's for you.

Serves 4

4 large aubergines, cut into 1.5cm chunks
10 medium tomatoes, cut in half
10 garlic cloves (skin on)
200ml veg oil, plus extra for roasting the veg
4 tsp cumin seeds
A large bunch of coriander, stalks and leaves separated and finely chopped
2 bay leaves
2 red onions, sliced into half-moons
A thumb-sized piece of ginger, grated
2 tsp ground coriander
2 tsp chilli flakes
2 tbsp tomato purée
1 tsp sugar
1 tsp ground turmeric
1 tsp garam masala
Salt

Preheat the oven to 180°C.

Place the aubergine chunks flat in a couple of roasting tins, sprinkle generously with salt on both sides and set aside for 10 minutes. In another roasting tin, lay out the tomatoes (cut-side down) and garlic cloves (in their skins), and cover generously with drizzled oil and sprinkled salt.

Once the salt has worked its magic and softened the aubergines slightly, drizzle them generously with oil. Then roast the aubergines and tomatoes and garlic in the oven for 45 minutes–1 hour until they're soft and caramelised.

When your veg is nearly cooked, heat the oil in a large frying pan on a medium heat. When it's hot, add the cumin seeds, coriander stalks (watch out for spitting oil) and bay leaves. Fry until the seeds are golden and the coriander stalks have turned a darker shade of green. Add the onions and ½ teaspoon of salt and turn the heat down low to cook the onions really slowly. When the onions begin to soften, add the ginger, ground coriander, chilli flakes, tomato purée and sugar, and cook until the onions are completely soft and caramelised (10–15 minutes in total).

When the aubergines, tomatoes and garlic are cooked, pop the garlic from their skins, then add them to the onion mix along with the tomatoes and aubergines. Squish the tomatoes and garlic with the back of your wooden spatula so they dissolve into the sauce. Add the turmeric and a cup of water and simmer for 5 minutes. Finish by stirring through the coriander leaves and garam masala. Taste for seasoning.

KERALAN BLACK-EYED BEAN & PUMPKIN CURRY

I first ate this dish while staying with a family on the backwaters of Kerala. Every night I'd stand in the kitchen with a notebook as our host cooked up the most delicious meals. This dish particularly stood out as I'd never eaten black-eyed beans in the context of Indian food. This dish is called 'Olan' and is eaten as part of the harvest festival feasts. If you can't find black-eyed beans, then black or cannellini beans would work.

Serves 2

½ a medium-sized pumpkin or butternut squash, deseeded and cut into 2.5cm chunks (leave the skin on)

Veg oil, for roasting the veg

1½ tbsp coconut oil

1½ tsp brown mustard seeds

1 cassia bark or cinnamon stick

4 cloves

1 green chilli, slit lengthways

10 fresh curry leaves (optional, leave out if you can't find fresh)

1 medium white onion, sliced into half-moons

2 large garlic cloves, crushed

A thumb-sized piece of ginger, grated

1 × 400g tin of black-eyed beans, drained and rinsed

½ tsp ground turmeric

½ tsp ground black pepper

1 tsp sugar

1 × 400ml tin of coconut milk

A large handful of spinach

Juice of ½ lemon

Salt

A small bunch of fresh coriander (stalks included), roughly chopped, to garnish

A handful of coconut flakes, toasted (page 38), to garnish

Preheat the oven to 200°C. Place the pumpkin or squash chunks in a roasting tin, drizzle with veg oil and sprinkle with a generous pinch of salt. Roast in the oven until the skin is golden brown and the flesh is soft (about 30 minutes).

While your pumpkin is roasting, heat the coconut oil in a large frying pan on a medium heat. Add the mustard seeds, cassia bark or cinnamon stick and cloves, and fry until the seeds begin to pop. Add the chilli and curry leaves, and fry until they begin to crisp up. Add the onion and 1 teaspoon of salt and turn the heat down low to cook the onion really slowly. When the onion begins to soften – after about 5 minutes – add the garlic and ginger, and cook until the onion is completely soft and caramelised (10–15 minutes in total).

Add the black-eyed beans and roasted pumpkin or squash to the pan and sprinkle over the turmeric, pepper and sugar. Stir until it is all well coated with the onion mix. Add the coconut milk, turn the heat up to bring the pan to a simmer, then let it cook on low for about 10 minutes until the beans have softened and the sauce has reduced a little. You can always add a little water at this stage if you think it needs to be saucier.

When the curry is done, stir through the spinach until it has wilted down. Take the pan off the heat and stir through the lemon juice. Taste for seasoning. Serve topped with the coriander and coconut flakes.

If I could only eat one meal for the rest of my life, it would be dhal. I'm happy to narrow that down further, to a steaming bowl of classic red lentil tarka dhal – no rice or bread needed but perhaps the luxury of a pickled pink onion and sprinkling of fresh coriander on top.

It feels like dhal is having a much-deserved renaissance at the moment, partly thanks to the Instagram wellness tribe and partly thanks to the new wave of amazing, plant-led cooks and writers whose various pulse-based recipes spring up almost weekly on the pages of weekend newspapers and social media feeds (a special shout-out to two of my faves, Anna Jones and Meera Sodha).

Trends aside, dhal deserves nothing less than its own chapter in this book. It can stake a claim to being the holy trinity of cheap, nutritious and easy to make – it's almost impossible to mess up (at least it will be once you're done with this chapter!). Read on for a foolproof method for classic tarka dhal as well as some jazzier numbers to impress your friends and family with.

TARKA DHAL

This is a very simple classic dhal recipe. But don't be fooled by its simplicity – when done right, this is one of my favourite dhals to eat. Much of the credit for this recipe should go to Rupal Acharya, who ran our kitchen during the street food days of SpiceBox. She helped me create it in the run up to the British Dhal Festival in 2018. To our delight, it won us the Best Dhal in Britain award! The secret to this dish is to cook the onions low and slow until they are soft and sweet. Also, don't hold back with the salt as it really lifts the dish. *Pictured overleaf*

Serves 4 as a side/2 as a main

200g split red lentils
½ tsp ground turmeric
4 tbsp veg oil
1 large white onion, sliced into
    half-moons
4 large garlic cloves, grated
    or crushed
A thumb-sized piece of ginger,
    grated
1½ tbsp cumin seeds
10 fresh curry leaves (optional,
    leave out if you can't find fresh)
2 green chillies, slit lengthways
Salt
A small bunch of coriander (stalks
    included), roughly chopped
A pinch of chilli flakes (optional)
A pinch of Pink Onion Pickle
    (page 228 – optional)

First, rinse the lentils. The best way to do this is by putting them in a large bowl, covering with cold water and then gently swirling them around with your hands until the water becomes cloudy. Drain and repeat at least three times until the water is clear.

Place them in a medium saucepan with the turmeric and ½ teaspoon of salt. Cover with 600ml cold water and bring to the boil. Simmer for around 20 minutes until the lentils are soft but still have a bit of shape and bite.

While the lentils are cooking, heat 2 tablespoons of the oil in a large frying pan on a medium heat. When the oil is hot, add the onion with a generous pinch of salt, and turn the heat down low to cook the onion really slowly. When the onion begins to soften – after about 5 minutes – add the garlic and ginger, and cook until the onion is completely soft and caramelised (10–15 minutes in total).

In a separate small frying pan, heat the remaining 2 tablespoons of oil on a medium heat. When it's hot, add the cumin seeds, curry leaves and green chillies, and cook until the seeds turn golden and all the delicious aromas are released.

Add the onions and spice mix to the lentils and stir. Taste for seasoning – remember that dhal loves salt!

Serve topped with the coriander and chilli flakes and Pink Onion Pickle, if using.

DHAL UPGRADES

Once you've mastered the basic dhal recipe, it's time to pimp up your dhal! Use the Tarka Dhal recipe on the opposite page as the base, then use the chart to help you get creative.

Flavour boosters

Coconut milk: Add ¼–½ of a 400ml tin to the lentils pan just before you add the spice and onion mix. This will loosen the dhal, so if you want it thicker just boil it for a bit longer to reduce down.

Lemon juice and zest: Once you've taken the cooked dhal off the heat, add the juice of ½ lemon and a few grates of zest.

Coriander seeds: Add 1 tsp of crushed coriander seeds when you fry the cumin seeds.

Fennel seeds: Add 1 tsp of fennel seeds when you fry the cumin seeds.

Mustard seeds: Add 1 tsp of brown mustard seeds when you fry the cumin seeds.

Tomatoes: Add 2 diced tomatoes to the saucepan with the raw lentils.

Garam masala: Stir through 1 tsp of garam masala once you've taken your cooked dhal off the heat.

Veg combos

Carrot and coriander: Add 2 roughly diced carrots to the saucepan with the raw lentils. Stir through a roughly chopped bunch of coriander just before you take the cooked dhal off the heat.

Cabbage and fennel: Add ¼ cabbage and ½ fennel bulb, both thinly sliced, to the onions when you add the garlic and ginger, and cook until soft.

Sweet potato and kale: Add chunks of roasted sweet potato and shredded kale to the dhal just after you've added the onions and spice mix, and cook until the kale has wilted.

Spinach and peas: Just before you take your cooked dhal off the heat, stir through a large handful of chopped spinach and 2 handfuls of frozen peas. Finish with a squeeze of lemon

Toppings

Coconut yoghurt and nigella (black onion) seeds: Add a dollop of coconut yoghurt sprinkled with a pinch of nigella seeds.

Crispy shallots: See page 27.

Spring Radish Pickle: See page 231.

Fried curry leaves: Fry 10 fresh curry leaves in 2 tbsp of oil until they crisp up, and pour them over your finished bowl of dhal.

Chilli oil: Add 2 tbsp of veg oil to a small frying pan. When it's hot, add 1 tsp of chilli flakes and 1 tsp of chilli powder. Then pour over your bowl of dhal.

Toasted cashew nuts or flaked almonds: See page 38.

Toasted coconut flakes: See page 38.

Toasted desiccated coconut: Follow the same method for toasted coconut flakes on page 38.

Toasted sunflower seeds: See page 38.

Chopped Spicy Nuts: See page 171.

Sliced green chillies: See page 36.

Pink Onion Pickle: See page 228.

Coconut Chutney: See page 220.

DOLLY'S DHAL

My great aunt Dolly is the source of my love for India and its cuisine. Dolly met my great uncle Pea while he was living in Delhi. They fell in love, got married and eventually moved back to the UK in the 1990s, when I was a young child. Visits to Dolly and Pea's house were my first experience of the delights of Indian food. I remember the distinctive smell of simmering dhal and pilau rice as soon as we opened the door to their house – hints of the feast that we would be treated to later in the day.

After Pea died, Dolly moved to London and I now pay regular visits to her flat to imbue her life wisdom and, of course, spend some time in her kitchen. Dolly has never written down a recipe – instead, I must watch her closely, frantically typing notes on my phone, as she conjures up her culinary magic. This is her go-to dhal – just how I remember it from my childhood.

Serves 4 as a side/2 as a main

200g split red lentils
½ tsp ground turmeric
2 garlic cloves, finely diced
A thumb-sized piece of ginger, grated
2 large tomatoes, roughly chopped
2 green chillies, slit lengthways
2 tbsp veg oil
2 tsp brown mustard seeds
1 medium white onion, sliced into half-moons
1 dried red chilli, ripped in half
Salt
A small bunch of coriander, roughly chopped (stalks included), to garnish

First, rinse the lentils. The best way to do this is by putting them in a large bowl, covering with cold water and then gently swirling them around with your hands until the water becomes cloudy. Drain and repeat at least three times until the water is clear.

Place them in a medium saucepan and cover with 600ml water. Add the turmeric, garlic, ginger, fresh tomatoes, green chillies and ½ teaspoon of salt and bring to the boil. Skim off any foam that rises to the surface. Simmer for around 20 minutes until the lentils are thick and soft. Dolly likes to mash hers a little with the back of a wooden spatula.

While the lentils are cooking, heat the oil in a medium frying pan and add the mustard seeds. When they begin to pop, add the onion and dried red chilli, followed by a pinch of salt. Fry on a low heat until the onion is completely soft and caramelised (around 10–15 minutes).

When the lentils are cooked, add the onion mix to the saucepan and stir through. Taste for seasoning and add more salt if needed. Top with the coriander.

CHANA DHAL

Chana dhal is the name for split chickpeas, which have a distinctive nutty flavour. If you can't find them in your supermarket, they are available online or in Asian shops. Failing this, you can use yellow split peas, which have a similar texture.

Serves 4 as a side/2 as a main

180g chana dhal or yellow split peas
2 medium tomatoes, roughly chopped
A thumb-sized piece of ginger, grated
4 large garlic cloves, finely chopped
½ tsp ground turmeric
1 tsp chilli powder
1 tsp paprika
2 tbsp veg oil
1 tbsp cumin seeds
1 dried red chilli, ripped in half
A small bunch of coriander, roughly chopped (stalks included)
1 tsp garam masala
Salt

Soak the chana dhal for at least 8 hours, then rinse them in a bowl of cold water at least three times until the water is clear. Place in a large saucepan and cover with 1 litre of cold water, and add the fresh tomatoes, ginger, garlic, ground spices and ½ teaspoon of salt. Bring the water to the boil and cook the chana until it is soft – this will take at least an hour on a medium simmer. You may need to top up the water while it is cooking.

Just before you are ready to serve, make the temper. Heat the oil in a small frying pan on a medium heat and add the cumin seeds. Fry until golden and aromatic, then add the dried chilli and most of the chopped coriander (watch out for spitting oil). Finish with the garam masala and a generous pinch of salt.

Stir the temper mix through the cooked chickpeas. Serve in a bowl topped with the remaining coriander.

A NOTE ON TEMPERING

'Tempering' is the term used to describe frying whole spices and other aromatics, such as whole chillies, ginger and garlic, in hot oil. This cooking technique helps to release the oils from the spices, significantly increasing their flavour. Learning how to temper spices will really raise your dhal game. The secret is getting the temperature of the oil just right before adding the spices – the best way to do this is by testing the temperature by dropping a tiny bit of spice in first. You want the spice to fizzle when it hits the oil but not turn too dark too quickly. The perfect oil temperature will turn the spice golden brown in around 30 seconds.

Often when I am in a hurry, I'll boil up some split red lentils with salt and a teaspoon of turmeric. When they're nearly cooked, I'll heat some oil in a frying pan and temper a few teaspoons of whatever whole spices I have to hand (cumin seeds, coriander seeds, fennel seeds, nigella seeds etc.) with some sliced garlic and ginger. When the lentils are cooked, I'll pour the tempered spices over the dhal, with a pinch of salt and give it all a stir. This is a fail-safe quick dhal method.

MAKHANi DHAL

This creamy black dhal was cooked by one of our curry house chefs, Oli, as a special one week and went down a treat! It's definitely one to bring out for special occasions or to convince a sceptical carnivore that plant-based food can be super-luxurious.

Soaking the black gram for a minimum of 12 hours is essential. You can use tinned or dried kidney beans. Dried would also need soaking overnight before being well boiled for an hour or so. In terms of quantities, 80g dried beans makes about 20g cooked. However, I think tinned beans work just as well and are far less hassle – you need most of a standard-sized tin once drained. If you can't find the black gram, you can swap them out for brown lentils, but just note that the amount of water may need to be reduced and they won't need soaking.

Serves 6 as a side / 4 as a main

185g whole black gram
   (whole urad)
200g cooked kidney beans,
   drained and rinsed
1 tsp hot chilli powder
1 tsp paprika
2 tbsp veg oil
1 tbsp cumin seeds
2 green chillies, slit lenthways
1 medium white onion, diced
6 garlic cloves, grated or crushed
A thumb-sized piece of ginger,
   grated
2 tbsp dried fenugreek leaves
2 medium tomatoes, roughly
   chopped
½ tsp ground turmeric
2 tsp garam masala
3 tbsp oat or soya cream,
   plus 1 tbsp to garnish
Juice of ½ lemon
Salt
A small bunch of coriander
   (stalks included), roughly
   chopped, to garnish

The night before you want to cook, rinse the black gram in a bowl of cold water at least three times until the water is clear. Then cover with cold water and leave to soak for at least 12 hours.

When you are ready to cook, put the black gram, kidney beans, chilli powder, paprika, 1 teaspoon of salt and 850ml water into a large saucepan. Cover and cook on a medium heat for 1 hour 20 minutes.

After 30 minutes of cooking, make the temper. Heat the oil in a large frying pan on a medium heat. Add the cumin seeds and green chillies and fry until golden. Add the onion with a generous pinch of salt, and turn the heat down low to cook it really slowly. When the onion begins to soften – after about 5 minutes – add the garlic, ginger and fenugreek leaves, and cook until the onion is completely soft and caramelised (10–15 minutes in total). Turn up the heat and add the fresh tomatoes and turmeric, and cook until they begin to break down. Add the mix to the simmering lentils.

Continue to cook the dhal until the lentils and beans are super-soft. You may need to top up the pan with some water. Add the garam masala and cook for 5 minutes. Take the pan off the heat and stir through the oat cream and lemon juice. Taste for seasoning. Pour into a bowl and top with the coriander and a swirl of oat cream. Serve with Spring Radish Pickle (page 231).

15-MINUTE ONE-POT DHAL

This is a dish I turn to again and again – often when I'm too tired or busy to cook but want something filling, nutritious and super-tasty. If you're new to Indian cooking, or making dhals, then this recipe is a great place to start.

Serves 2 as a main

200g split red lentils
2 tbsp veg oil
2 tsp cumin seeds
1 green chilli, slit lengthways
3 garlic cloves, crushed with
  the side of your knife
A thumb-sized piece of ginger,
  finely diced
½ white onion, sliced into
  half-moons
2 tomatoes, roughly diced
800ml boiling water
½ tsp ground turmeric
Salt
A pinch of chilli flakes, to garnish
1 tbsp coconut yoghurt, to garnish
  (optional)

First, rinse the lentils. The best way to do this is by putting them in a large bowl, covering with cold water and then gently swirling them around with your hands until the water becomes cloudy. Drain and repeat at least three times until the water is clear. Set them to one side.

Place a medium saucepan on a medium heat and add the oil. When it's hot, add the cumin seeds, green chilli, garlic and ginger, and fry for a few minutes until everything is golden and smelling delicious. Now add the onion, fresh tomatoes and ½ teaspoon of salt and stir well.

Add the lentils to the saucepan, followed by the boiling water and the turmeric. Bring to the boil, then turn down the heat and simmer for 10–15 minutes until the lentils are soft but still have a bit of bite to them. Once the dhal is cooked, taste for seasoning – it may need a touch more salt.

Serve topped with the chilli flakes and a spoonful of coconut yoghurt, if using. If I have some toasted nuts or seeds lying around, I often add these too for texture.

CARROT & KALE MOONG DHAL

Mung beans are often hailed as the most nutritious of the pulses. I find that a steaming bowl of this dhal on a cold winter's day when I'm feeling a bit under the weather is the perfect pick-me-up. The carrots add a delicious sweetness and the kale some texture, but you can always sub them out for other veg you have lying around, such as sweet potato or spinach.

Serves 4–5 as a main

400g whole mung beans
5 tbsp veg oil
6 large garlic cloves, roughly chopped
A large thumb-sized piece of ginger, thinly sliced
2 green chillies, slit lengthways
1 tsp ground coriander
1 tsp ground turmeric
3 carrots, roughly diced
3 large handfuls of kale, roughly shredded (tough stalks removed)
2 tsp cumin seeds
2 tsp brown mustard seeds
1 tsp chilli flakes
Juice of ½ lemon
Salt

The night before you want to cook, rinse the mung beans in a bowl of cold water at least three times until the water is clear – look out for any stones or grit and remove them. Then cover with cold water and leave to soak for at least 12 hours.

When you are ready to cook, rinse the soaked mung beans again in cold water and set to one side.

Place a large saucepan on a medium heat and add 2 tablespoons of the oil. When it's hot, add the garlic, ginger, green chilies and ground coriander, and fry for a few minutes until the smell of raw garlic has gone. Add the mung beans, 1 litre of cold water, the turmeric and 1 teaspoon of salt, and bring to the boil. Simmer for about 50 minutes until the beans are soft but still have some body.

Halfway through the cooking, add the carrots. When your dhal is very nearly done, stir through the kale and simmer for 3–5 minutes until it's nice and soft. You can always add more water it you like your dhal thinner.

Take the dhal off the heat and make the temper. Heat the remaining 3 tablespoons of oil in a small frying pan and add the cumin and mustard seeds. Fry until they begin to pop, then add the chilli flakes. Stir the hot spiced oil into the dhal, followed by a generous pinch of salt. Finish by stirring through the lemon juice and taste for seasoning.

KiTCHARi

Ahhhh kitchari, the godmother of all comfort foods. Kitchari means 'mixture' in Hindi, which nods to the mix of rice and lentils in this dhal. In Ayurvedic medicine, kitchari is hailed as the dish that is suitable for all constitutions (doshas). It can easily be adapted to suit individual tastes – different vegetables can be added and you can increase or decrease the amount of water depending on whether you prefer yours thick and creamy or light and brothy. Mung dhal is the name for the split and skinned version of whole mung beans.

Serves 4–5 as a main

300g mung dhal
150g white basmati rice
2 tbsp coconut oil
1 cassia bark or cinnamon stick
4 cardamom pods, lightly crushed
3 cloves
2 tsp cumin seeds
1 tsp brown mustard seeds
1 tsp fennel seeds
1 tsp cracked black pepper
3 garlic cloves, roughly chopped
A large thumb-sized piece of
    ginger, thinly sliced
1½ tsp ground turmeric
3 carrots, roughly diced
3 large handfuls of spinach
Juice of 1 lemon
Salt
A small bunch of coriander,
    roughly chopped (stalks
    included), to garnish
A handful of toasted cashew nuts,
    to garnish

Start by rinsing the mung dhal and rice. The best way to do this is by putting them in a large bowl, covering with cold water and then gently swirling them around with your hands until the water becomes cloudy. Drain and repeat at least three times until the water is clear. Set to one side.

Heat the oil in a large saucepan on a medium heat and add all the whole spices and cracked pepper. Fry until the seeds are golden and aromatic. Now add the garlic and ginger, and fry for a couple of minutes. Add the washed mung dhal and rice, and stir. Cover with 1.5 litres of water and then add the turmeric, 1 teaspoon of salt and carrots. Turn up the heat to bring it to the boil. When it is bubbling away, turn down the heat and simmer gently for at least 40 minutes – you want the dhal and rice to be super-soft, almost like porridge. You can always add more water at this stage if you want a thinner consistency.

Take the kitchari off the heat and stir through the spinach, lemon juice and a generous pinch of salt. Taste for seasoning. Serve topped with the coriander and toasted cashews. I also sometimes eat mine with a dollop of creamy coconut yoghurt.

AUNTiE DOLLY'S KiTCHARi

When I go to visit my Auntie Dolly, we often end up in the kitchen together – me watching her rustle up something for me to take home. During one of these kitchen sessions, while making me a dhal of some sort, she began to recite her recipe for kitchari. Like most good home cooks, Dolly has no recipes written down, so I whipped out my phone and began to make notes – the result is the below. Perhaps not 100% accurate to Dolly's verbal recipe but it tastes amazing, nonetheless.

Serves 4–5 as a main

300g split red lentils

150g white basmati rice

6 tbsp veg oil

3 cloves

1 medium white onion, sliced into half-moons

6 garlic cloves, crushed with the side of your knife

A large thumb-sized piece of ginger, thinly sliced

1 tsp ground coriander

2 tomatoes, roughly chopped

1 tsp ground turmeric

2 tsp cumin seeds

2 tsp brown mustard seeds

70g cashew nuts, roughly chopped

2 dried red chillies, ripped into quarters

Juice of 1 lemon

Salt

First, rinse the lentils and rice. The best way to do this is by putting them in a large bowl, covering with cold water and then gently swirling them around with your hands until the water becomes cloudy. Drain and repeat at least three times until the water is clear. Set to one side.

Heat 3 tablespoons of the oil in a large saucepan on a medium heat and add the cloves, onion, 1 teaspoon of salt, garlic, ginger and ground coriander. Fry for a few minutes until the mix starts to turn golden, then add the fresh tomatoes and turmeric and stir. Add the rinsed lentils and rice and cover with 1.5 litres of cold water. Turn up the heat to bring it to the boil. When it is bubbling away, turn down the heat and simmer gently for at least 40 minutes – you want the lentils and rice to be super-soft, almost like porridge.

When the kitchari is cooked, take it off the heat and make the temper. Heat the remaining 3 tablespoons of oil in a small frying pan and add the cumin seeds, mustard seeds and cashews. Fry until the seeds begin to pop and then add the dried chillies. Continue frying until the cashews turn golden, then add the temper mix to the kitchari and stir. Finish by adding the lemon juice and a generous pinch of salt.

LiME & COCONUT DHAL

You may not immediately think to cook up a bowl of dhal on a hot summer's day but this creamy, zesty dhal works really well as a light summertime dinner. The lime and coconut give it a tropical edge and really help to bring out the flavour of the spices.

Serves 4 as a side/2 as a main

200g split red lentils
¼ tsp ground turmeric
2 large garlic cloves, grated
   or crushed
A thumb-sized piece of ginger,
   grated
1 green chilli, slit lengthways
75ml coconut milk
1 tbsp coconut oil
1 tsp brown mustard seeds
10 fresh curry leaves (optional,
   leave out if you can't find fresh)
1 tsp garam masala
2 limes, zest and juice of 1, plus 1
   cut into wedges to serve
Salt
A small bunch of coriander,
   roughly chopped (stalks
   included), to garnish
Toasted coconut flakes
   (page 38), to garnish

First, rinse the lentils. The best way to do this is by putting them in a large bowl, covering with cold water and then gently swirling them around with your hands until the water becomes cloudy. Drain and repeat at least three times until the water is clear.

Place them in a large saucepan and cover with 600ml water. Add the turmeric, garlic, ginger, chilli and ½ teaspoon of salt, and bring to the boil. Simmer for around 20 minutes until the lentils are soft. You want the dhal to be thick at this stage so resist adding water. When the dhal is cooked, stir through the coconut milk and take off the heat.

Once the dhal is cooked, make the spice temper. Heat the oil in a small frying pan on a medium heat and add the mustard seeds and curry leaves. Once the seeds begin to pop and the curry leaves have crisped up, add the garam masala and fry for 1 minute. Take the pan off the heat and add the temper immediately to the dhal, along with a generous pinch of salt. Stir through the lime zest and juice and taste for seasoning.

Serve in a bowl, topped with coriander, coconut flakes and a wedge of lime.

GRAINS
& BREADS

An Indian meal isn't complete without a grain of some sort – be it a steaming bowl of basmati rice or a soft, freshly cooked roti.

In this chapter, you'll find a foolproof method for cooking perfect basmati rice, but I'll also deviate from curry-house tradition by exploring some alternative spins on grain dishes.

Indian flavours and cooking methods lend themselves to more adventurous grain dishes. The variety of grains on offer at supermarkets is growing and, at home, I often find myself swapping out rice for quinoa or pearl barley when making a pilau, or serving a bowl of dhal alongside a freekeh salad.

One thing that unites all these dishes, however, is simplicity. That's why you won't find a paratha or traditional biriyani recipe in this chapter. Delicious as they are, some things are best saved for a meal out or for when you're being cooked for by a more talented Indian home cook than you or I. Having said that, your local Asian store will usually have a very decent ready-made packet of parathas in their freezer.

THE PERFECT BASMATI RICE

Cooking perfect rice requires patience and precision. If you follow the recipe below carefully, I guarantee you will have perfect rice every time.

Serves 4

400g dry white basmati rice
  (I really recommend using Tilda
  as the quality of own-brand
  supermarket stuff really varies)
2 cloves
2 cardamom pods, lightly crushed
½ tsp fine sea salt
1 tbsp veg oil

Start by rinsing your rice. The best way to do this is by putting the dry rice in a large bowl, covering it with cold water and then gently swirling it around with your hands until the water becomes cloudy. Drain and repeat at least three times until the water is clear.

Place the washed rice in a saucepan and cover it with water. Leave to soak for 15 minutes.

Drain the rice, put it back in the saucepan and cover with 600ml cold water. Add the cloves, cardamom, salt and oil. Cover the pan with a tightly fitting lid and bring it to a rapid boil – if your lid isn't transparent you can tell by listening out for bubbling water and looking for lots of steam.

As soon as the water is boiling, turn off the heat – do not remove the lid! Leave the saucepan to stand, with the lid on, for 40 minutes.

After 40 minutes (not a minute before!), take the lid off and gently run a fork through the rice to fluff it up.

For the ultimate basmati rice, serve topped with crispy shallots (page 27).

COCONUT RICE

This is such an easy way to give your rice a luxurious lift. Coconut rice is great with some of the spicier recipes in this book, as the creaminess helps to offset the heat from chillies. It's especially good with the Jackfruit Jalfrezi on pages 74–6.

Serves 4

200g jasmine rice
½ tbsp coconut oil
2 cloves
2 cardamom pods, crushed
200ml coconut milk
½ tsp fine sea salt

Start by rinsing your rice. The best way to do this is by putting the dry rice in a large bowl, covering it with cold water and then gently swirling it around with your hands until the water becomes cloudy. Drain and repeat at least three times until the water is clear.

Rub the oil over the bottom of a saucepan and add the rice, cloves, cardamom, coconut milk, salt and 200ml water. Bring to the boil, stirring occasionally to stop the rice from sticking to the bottom of the pan. Once the mixture is bubbling away, turn the heat down and place a lid on top. Simmer gently for 5 minutes until most of the liquid has been absorbed by the rice – you will need to stir it from time to time to stop it sticking.

Take the pan off the heat, leaving the lid on. Leave it to sit for 5 minutes. Fluff up the rice with a fork before serving.

THREE-GRAIN PiLAU

This is a recipe I turn to again and again. In fact, I can't remember the last time I ate a grain that wasn't fried in salty-sweet caramelised onion and cumin seeds. Once you've mastered this recipe, you'll be well equipped to jazz up any grain in your cupboard – see the chart on page 134 for some tips.

Serves 4

100g dry pearl barley
55g dry quinoa
100g dry bulgur wheat
3 tbsp veg oil
3 cloves
1 cassia bark or cinnamon stick
2 bay leaves
1 tbsp cumin seeds
1 large white onion, sliced into
     half-moons
1 green chilli, slit lengthways
Salt

Start by rinsing your grains. The best way to do this is by putting each grain in a separate large bowl, covering with cold water and then gently swirling it around with your hands until the water becomes cloudy. Drain and repeat at least three times until the water is clear.

Put the pearl barley in a large saucepan and cover with 600ml water. Add 1 teaspoon of salt and bring to the boil. Simmer for 10 minutes.

While the pearl barley is cooking, heat the oil in a large frying pan and add the cloves, cassia bark or cinnamon stick, bay leaves and cumin seeds. Fry until the seeds turn golden, then add the onion, green chilli and 1 teaspoon of salt. Turn the heat down low and fry really slowly until the onion is completely soft and caramelised (10–15 minutes).

When the pearl barley has been simmering for 10 minutes, add the quinoa and cook for a further 10 minutes. Then add the bulgur wheat and simmer for 5 minutes.

When the grains are cooked, drain off any excess water and stir through the onion mix. Taste for seasoning.

BUiLD YOUR OWN PiLAU

Use the Three-Grain Pilau recipe as your starting point and customise it using some of the following possible combinations.

Serves 4

Spice

Fry 1–3 of the spices below in hot oil until golden and aromatic.

1 tbsp cumin seeds

2 tsp brown mustard seeds

1 cassia bark or cinnamon stick

2 bay leaves

3 cloves

1 tbsp nigella (black onion) seeds

2 tsp fennel seeds

2 tsp coriander seeds, crushed

4 cardamom pods, crushed

1 tsp black peppercorns

2 star anise

Base

Add 1–3 of the ingredients below with a generous pinch of salt.

1 large red onion, sliced into half-moons

1 large white onion, sliced into half-moons

4 large garlic cloves, grated or crushed

A thumb-sized piece of ginger, grated

2 green chillies, slit lengthways or sliced

2 tsp chilli flakes

2 dried red chillies, ripped into quarters

Grain

Stir the base into 1–3 cooked grains (500g in total) from the list below. See the packet label for individual cooking instructions.

Pearl barley

White basmati rice

Brown basmati rice

Short-grain brown rice

Short-grain white rice

Quinoa

Buckwheat

Freekeh

Bulgur wheat

Millet

Couscous

PiLAU RiCE

I have such fond memories of this aromatic golden-yellow rice –
it instantly takes me back to curry night at home when I was a kid.
A takeaway at the Regan house wasn't complete without a foil tray
of pilau to soak up the tikka masala, madras and dhal.

Serves 4

250g dry white basmati rice (try
   to buy the best quality you can
   find – I use Tilda)
2 tbsp unsweetened plant milk
   (I use almond)
A pinch of saffron
4 tbsp veg oil
4 cardamom pods, lightly crushed
1 cassia bark or cinnamon stick
4 cloves
4 black peppercorns
2 tsp cumin seeds
2 bay leaves
1 large white onion, sliced into
   half-moons
1 tsp fine sea salt

Start by rinsing your rice. The best way to do this is by putting the dry rice in a large bowl, covering it with cold water and then gently swirling it around with your hands until the water becomes cloudy. Drain and repeat at least three times until the water is clear.

Cover the rinsed rice one last time with cold water and leave to soak for 15 minutes.

Heat the milk in a microwave or saucepan until it's warm but not boiling. Take off the heat, add the saffron and set to one side to infuse.

Place a large frying pan or casserole dish with a tightly fitting lid on a medium heat. Add the oil and, when it's hot, add the whole spices and bay leaves. Fry them until they are golden and aromatic. Add the onion and salt, and turn the heat down low to cook the onion really slowly until it's completely soft and caramelised (10–15 minutes) – a super-soft, sweet onion is key to a great pilau.

When the onion is cooked, drain the rice and add it to the onion mix. Stir gently, being careful not to break the rice grains. Cover with 500ml cold water, then turn up the heat and bring to the boil. When the water is boiling, put on the lid and leave for 10 seconds before turning off the heat.

Leave the rice to stand in the covered pan for 40 minutes – do not remove the lid!

When the time is up, take the lid off and add the saffron milk. Use a fork to very gently mix in the milk and fluff up the rice.

Pilau rice tastes amazing topped with the crispy shallots on page 27.

CHEAT'S VEG BIRIYANI

A traditional biriyani takes hours to cook but this cheat's version can be ready in 30 minutes. It is a great way to use up leftover rice but can also be made with pouches of ready-cooked rice. If you don't have cooked rice, make a batch of The Perfect Basmati Rice on page 130 first.

Serves 4

½ cauliflower, in small florets
4 carrots, thinly sliced
3 tbsp veg oil, plus extra for roasting veg
150ml unsweetened almond milk
A large pinch of saffron
3 cardamom pods, crushed
1 cassia bark or cinnamon stick
2 cloves
2 bay leaves
1 tsp cumin seeds
1 medium white onion, sliced into half-moons
4 garlic cloves, grated or crushed
A thumb-sized piece of ginger, grated
1 green chilli, slit lengthways
2 medium tomatoes, roughly chopped
1 tbsp tomato purée
1 tsp sugar
1 tsp ground coriander
1 tsp chilli powder
100g green beans, topped and cut in half
100g Tenderstem broccoli, roughly chopped
600g cooked basmati rice (200g dry rice if cooking from scratch)
100g cashew nuts, roasted and roughly chopped
A medium bunch of coriander (including stalks), finely chopped
A medium bunch of mint (leaves only), finely chopped
1½ tsp garam masala
Salt

Start by roasting the veg. Preheat the oven to 200°C.

Place the cauliflower florets and sliced carrots in separate roasting tins, drizzle with oil and sprinkle with salt. Roast the cauliflower for around 30 minutes until it is charred and crispy on the outside and cooked through in the middle. Roast the carrots for around 20 minutes until they are soft but caramelised on the outside. Set the roasted veg to one side.

Next make the saffron milk. Put the milk on a gentle heat and add the saffron. Bring to a simmer for 5 minutes and then turn off the heat. Leave the milk to infuse while you start making the biriyani.

Heat the oil in a shallow cast-iron casserole dish or a large heavy-based frying pan on a medium heat and add the cardamom, cassia bark or cinnamon stick, cloves, bay leaves and cumin seeds. Fry for a minute until they are golden and aromatic. Add the onion and 1 teaspoon of salt and turn the heat down low to cook the onion really slowly. When the onion begins to soften – after about 5 minutes – add the garlic, ginger, green chilli and fresh tomatoes, and cook until the onion is completely soft and caramelised and the tomatoes have broken down (10–15 minutes).

Add the tomato purée, sugar, ground coriander and chilli powder, and stir-fry for a couple of minutes. Now add all the veg, followed by a generous pinch of salt. Stir well so it's all coated with the spiced onion mix. Then use the back of your wooden spatula to flatten the veg so it forms a tightly packed layer on the bottom of the pan. Cover the veg with half the cooked rice, again tightly packing it down with the back of your spatula. Top with half the cashews, half the coriander and half the mint. Spoon over half the saffron milk – you want to dot it evenly over the surface of the rice. Finish by sprinkling over half the garam masala and a pinch of salt.

Repeat this process for the second layer of rice, packing down rice, cashews, coriander and mint, spooning over the remaining milk and finishing with garam masala and a pinch of salt.

Cover the pan with a lid and cook on a low heat for 5 minutes. Serve straight from the pan with the Raita on page 232.

INDIAN FRIED RICE

This is a great way of using up any leftover cooked rice. Feel free to switch up the veg – I tend to use what I've got lying around the bottom of my fridge but fast-cooking vegetables work best here.

I usually use basmati rice for this recipe, but it would work with any cooked rice or grain. If you don't have any cooked rice, follow the recipe for The Perfect Basmati Rice (page 130) and make yourself a batch first.

Serves 2 as a main/4 as a side

3 tbsp sesame or veg oil
4 cloves
2 tsp cumin seeds
2 tsp brown mustard seeds
2 green chillies, slit lengthways
10 fresh curry leaves or 2 bay leaves
1 tsp chilli flakes
1 medium white onion, sliced into half-moons
6 garlic cloves, thinly sliced
2 large handfuls of assorted prepped veg (I like to use thinly sliced red pepper, sugar snap peas and Tenderstem broccoli – make sure you thinly slice any large veg that will take longer to cook)
320g cooked rice (150g dry rice if cooking from scratch)
1 tsp ground turmeric
1 tsp garam masala
A medium bunch of coriander, roughly chopped (stalks included)
100g toasted cashew nuts, roughly chopped
Salt
A small bunch of spring onions, thinly sliced, to garnish
1 lime, quartered, to garnish

Heat the oil in a large frying pan or wok on a medium heat and add the cloves, cumin and mustard seeds. Fry until they begin to pop, then add the green chillies, curry or bay leaves and chilli flakes. Add the onion and 1 teaspoon of salt, and fry until the onion starts to soften – about 5 minutes. Then add the garlic and all the veg (you can add the veg in stages if some will take a bit longer to cook than others) – keep stirring while they cook.

When the veg is nearly cooked, add the rice, turmeric and garam masala and stir well. When the rice is warmed through, take the pan off the heat and stir through most of the coriander and cashews. Taste for seasoning.

Serve topped with the sliced spring onion, a sprinkling of toasted cashews and coriander and a wedge of lime on the side.

NAAN

I'm unfortunately not yet the owner of a tandoor oven, though I certainly plan to be one day. If you're the lucky owner of a pizza oven or perhaps even a tandoor (congratulations on living your best life), I certainly recommend cooking these naans in it.

I'd always thought that perfect fluffy-on-the-inside and bubbly-and-charred-on-the-outside naans were out of the question until I reached the momentous day when I had acquired said wood-fired oven. However, I was determined to put an achievable naan recipe in this book. After some testing, I landed on this recipe and I can't quite believe how great they turn out. If, like me, you're not a super-experienced baker, fear not – these are very simple to make.

If you don't fancy a 5-minute workout, you can use a food mixer with a dough hook to knead the dough (set at a high speed for 5 minutes). If you don't have a food mixer, it is also possible to knead the dough using a food processor, simply place the dry ingredients in the processor with the standard blade attachment and turn it on to a low speed setting. Slowly add the water until the dough comes together. Once it's formed a ball, keep it moving for a minute before leaving it to rest.

Makes 6 small breads

¾ tsp dried yeast
125ml lukewarm water
250g strong white bread flour,
    plus extra for dusting
½ tbsp fine sea salt
3 tbsp veg oil, plus extra for
    brushing the cooked breads
3 tbsp plain unsweetened soya
    yoghurt (I use Alpro)

Ingredients cont. page 142

Combine the yeast and water in a bowl and set aside for 5 minutes.

Put the flour and salt in a large mixing bowl and make a well in the middle. Pour the oil, yoghurt and yeast mixture into the well. Using a fork, gradually bring the flour into the centre from the sides of the well and mix until a rough dough is formed. It should be quite wet and sticky so add more water if you think it needs it.

Transfer the dough to a floured surface and knead for around 5 minutes, or until it's smooth. Lightly oil a bowl and put the ball of dough in it. Cover with a clean tea towel or clingfilm and leave for a minimum of 1½ hours (up to 8 hours) in a warm place. It will increase in size during this time.

Recipe cont. page 142

1 tbsp nigella (black onion) seeds
Sea salt flakes, to taste

Preheat the oven to 80°C.

Once the dough has risen, knock it back with your hands and then divide it into six balls. On a well-floured surface, roll one ball into an oval around 1cm thick – don't worry if it isn't neat.

Heat a dry, heavy-based frying pan on a high heat. When it's really hot, add the naan and cook on one side until it starts to bubble (around 3 minutes). Flip it over and cook until the other side is nicely browned and the bread is cooked through.

When the bread is still hot, brush it lightly with oil and add a sprinkling of nigella seeds. Finish with a pinch of sea salt flakes.

Repeat this process for each dough ball, keeping the naans warm in the oven until you are ready to serve.

PURi

Puris are essentially deep-fried roti. Plunging the raw dough discs in hot oil makes them puff up into pillows – soft and light in the middle and crispy on the outside. They may seem technical but if I can do it, I promise you can too (I'm by no means an experienced or talented baker).

As with the Naan (page 140), you can knead by hand or use a food mixer with a dough hook, or even a food processor. *Pictured overleaf*

Makes 16 small breads

350g wholemeal flour, plus extra
　for dusting
2 tsp fine sea salt
3 tbsp veg oil, plus extra for
　deep-frying – at least 500ml
250ml warm water

Put the flour into a large bowl with the salt and mix well. Gradually add the oil and warm water, mixing with a fork as you go. When all the liquid has been added and the dough starts to come together, transfer it onto a clean surface. You shouldn't need to flour your surface as the oil will stop the dough from sticking. However, if it does start to stick, feel free to add a dusting of flour. Knead for at least 5 minutes until the dough is firm and smooth.

Put the dough in a clean bowl and cover with clingfilm. Leave to rest for at least 30 minutes (up to 2 hours if you want).

Fill a large saucepan with oil – it needs to be at least 5cm deep. Place it on a high heat. You can test if the oil is the correct temperature by dropping a small piece of dough in it. If it floats to the surface quickly, the oil is ready. If you have a thermometer to hand, the oil should be 190–195°C. Make sure the oil doesn't get too hot – you don't want to burn the puri or cook them too quickly as they will stay raw in the middle.

Divide the dough into 16 small pieces. Use the palms of your hands to roll each piece into a smooth, neat ball. Flatten it slightly between your hands and place it onto a clean, lightly floured surface. Using a rolling pin, roll it into a thin round disc, around 9cm in diameter. The neater the balls are at the start, the easier it will be to make a circle.

Slide a dough disc flat into the oil. As soon as it rises to the surface, use the back of a slotted spoon to gently press it into the oil. It should start to blow up into a round balloon. Once it's golden on one side (around 3 minutes), flip it and cook until it's golden on the other side. If your discs don't puff up, the oil may not be hot enough.

Repeat with the remaining dough balls and place them on a tray lined with kitchen paper when they're done.

Serve them straight away. They can also be served cold, but nothing beats a warm puri fresh from the pan.

ROTi

This roti recipe is super-simple – but the secret to a good roti is in the kneading. Make sure you knead it well. If you're feeling lazy, you can use a food mixer with a dough hook, or even a food processor (see page 140).

Makes 8 roti

250g wholemeal flour, plus extra
   for dusting
1 tsp fine sea salt
170ml lukewarm water
Veg oil, for cooking the roti

Put the flour and salt in a large mixing bowl. Slowly add the water, using a fork to mix it in at the start.

As soon as the mixture begins to form a dough, transfer it onto a floured surface and knead well for 5 minutes until it becomes smooth and soft.

Put the dough back in the bowl and leave it to rest for 15 minutes, covered with a clean tea towel.

Preheat the oven to 80°C.

Place a dry, heavy-based frying pan on the highest heat you can. While it's getting smoking hot, divide the dough into eight balls and, using a rolling pin, roll them into circles (around 17cm in diameter and 2mm thick) on a floured surface.

When your pan is *really* hot, add a roti, and fry until it begins to brown and bubble on one side (around 3 minutes). Flip and repeat.

If you have a gas hob, finish off the roti directly on the open flame for a super-authentic charred and bubbly bread.

In between cooking the roti, lightly oil and wipe the pan with kitchen roll to keep it clean. Repeat the cooking process for each dough ball, keeping the roti warm in the oven until you are ready to serve.

STREET SNACKS

In India, street food stalls are part of the fabric of every city. They originated as a way to feed people who didn't have a kitchen in their own home, but they have since evolved into mini restaurants in their own right, welcoming anyone from rickshaw drivers to lawyers to eat at their kerbside.

Regardless of the city, season or time of day, on every street corner in India you will find satisfied customers popping delicate puri puffs filled with sweet-sour tamarind water, shovelling down aloo chaat from a banana leaf bowl or gnawing on blackened sweetcorn anointed with lashings of ghee, chilli and lime.

Although Indian cuisine doesn't really do 'starters', the street snack recipes found in the following pages make for the perfect appetiser before the main event. I also find myself throwing together various spins on a chaat for a light midweek lunch or dinner. Many of the accompanying sauces and chutneys can be kept in the fridge for weeks and pulled out to jazz up a simple salad or grain dish.

CHANA CHAAT

Chaat is a street food snack served on roadsides across India. There are many different varieties of chaats but most contain chopped onion, coriander, sev (fried chickpea noodles) and a yoghurt dressing. They have a perfect balance of freshness from the raw onion, crunch from the sev and creaminess from the yoghurt.

Chaats are traditionally spiced with chaat masala – a moreish blend of dried mango powder (also known as amchoor), cumin and black salt. Most Indian shops will sell this but it's tricky to find in supermarkets, so I've left it out of this recipe. If you do come across some, you can swap out the spices and salt below for 1 tablespoon of chaat masala.

Once you've nailed this chaat recipe, I encourage you to get creative. See the chaat chart opposite for tips on how you can create your own chaats.

Serves 4 as a starter/side

1 × 400g tin of chickpeas, drained and rinsed
1 tsp ground black pepper
½ tsp ground cinnamon
2 medium tomatoes, finely diced
1 medium cucumber, deseeded and finely diced
½ medium red onion, finely diced
A small bunch of mint (leaves only), finely chopped
A small bunch of coriander (stalks included), finely chopped
1 tbsp veg oil
1 tsp cumin seeds
Juice of 1 lime
1 tbsp sev (swap out for broken poppadum pieces if you can't find it)
Date and Tamarind Chutney (page 215)
Raita (page 232)
Salt

Place the chickpeas in a bowl with the black pepper, cinnamon and 1 teaspoon of salt. Leave to marinate while you prep your salad. Mix the tomatoes, cucumber, onion, mint and most of the coriander in a bowl.

Heat the oil in a frying pan on a medium heat and add the cumin seeds. When they're golden, add the spiced chickpeas and fry until they begin to crisp up. Take off the heat.

Season the salad with the lime juice and a generous pinch of salt. Spoon on to a plate and top with the spiced chickpeas and sev. Drizzle with Date and Tamarind Chutney and Raita and garnish with the remaining chopped coriander.

Tip – *Try swapping the Date and Tamarind Chutney and Raita for Coriander Chutney (page 213) for an amazing lunchtime salad.*

CHAAT CHART

Chaats make the most delicious lunch or light dinner and are a great way to use up any leftovers from a curry night. Use the chart below to build your own chaat. This is just a starting point and I encourage you get experimental!

Base
(pick 3–4)

Diced cucumber

Diced tomatoes

Diced onions

Diced boiled potatoes

Chickpeas

Puffed rice

Sprouted mung beans or lentils

Hero ingredient
(pick 1)

Speedy Samosas (broken into pieces – see page 172)

Aloo Tiki (page 160)

Spiced Crispy Chickpeas (page 174)

Pea Kachori (page 164)

Crispy Tofu 'Paneer' (page 200)

Pakora (page 156)

Chutneys
(pick 1–2)

Green Chutney (page 221)

Date and Tamarind Chutney (page 215)

Coriander Chutney (page 213)

Raita (page 232)

Toppings
(pick 2–3)

Sev

Crushed poppadums

Pink Onion Pickle (page 228)

Toasted cashew nuts or peanuts or almonds (page 38)

Sliced green chillies

Sliced raw red onion

ONION BHAJI

Onion bhajis usually come as balls of onion in a thick batter but I prefer my fried snacks super-light and crispy. The rice flour in this batter helps achieve this – and the result is a sort of cross between an onion bhaji and onion tempura.

Serves 4 as a starter/side

100g gram flour
50g rice flour
½ tsp ground turmeric
1 tbsp cumin seeds
2 green chillies, finely chopped
A small bunch of coriander (stalks included), finely chopped
Juice of ½ lemon
1 tsp fine sea salt, plus extra to taste
Veg oil, around 1 litre for frying
2 large white onions, thinly sliced into half-moons

Put the gram and rice flours in a large bowl and slowly whisk through 250ml water until a batter is formed. Stir through the rest of the ingredients, except the onions and veg oil. Your batter needs to be quite thin – the consistency of double cream – so add more water if you need to. A thinner batter leads to a crispier bhaji.

Pour the oil into a large saucepan or wok – it needs to be at least 5cm deep – and place on a high heat.

While the oil is heating up, mix the sliced onions into the batter, making sure that all the onion strands are separated.

Test the oil to make sure it is the right temperature by dropping a small piece of onion into it. It should fizz and turn golden brown in around 30 seconds. If you have a thermometer to hand, the oil should be 180°C.

Take a handful of battered onion and glide it across the surface of the oil. You want a thin web of bhaji rather than a ball. Fry until golden brown and then flip over with a slotted spoon (this will take around 1 minute 20 seconds on either side). When the other side is crisp and golden, use the spoon to remove the bhaji onto a plate covered with kitchen paper. Season generously with fine sea salt (I find this sticks to the bhaji better). Continue until all the onion has been fried.

You can keep the bhajis warm in a low oven while you cook the rest.

Serve with Mango and Apricot Chutney (page 222) or Date and Tamarind Chutney (page 215).

SEASONAL VEG PAKORA

On almost every city street in India, you'll find a food vendor tending to giant karahi of floating pakoras in bubbling oil. The battered veg varies depending on what's in season but soft, faster-cooking vegetables are preferable, such as onion, aubergine and spinach. I've listed seasonal veg and combinations that work well opposite. The harder the vegetable, the smaller you have to cut it. For root vegetables, grating works best.

Traditionally, just gram flour is used but I find adding rice flour and baking powder makes for a crisper batter at home.

For tips on pre-cooking veg, see pages 12–30. *Pictured overleaf*

Serves 4–6 as a starter/side

For the batter

Veg oil, around 1 litre for frying

100g gram flour

50g rice flour

½ tsp fine sea salt

2 tsp ajwain seeds (also called lovage or carom seeds; swap for fennel or nigella (black onion) seeds if you can't find them)

1 tsp cumin seeds

½ tsp ground turmeric

A thumb-sized piece of ginger, grated

1 green chilli, thinly sliced

A small bunch of coriander (stalks included), finely chopped

2 tsp garam masala

Salt

Pour the oil into a large saucepan or wok – it needs to be 5–7cm deep – and place on a high heat.

Put the gram and rice flours into a bowl, along with the rest of the batter ingredients. Slowly pour in 500ml water and whisk until a batter is formed – you're looking for the consistency of a thin pancake batter.

Test the oil to make sure it is the right temperature by dropping a piece of batter into it. It should fizzle and turn golden in around 30 seconds. If you have a thermometer to hand, the oil should be 180°C.

Drop a small handful of your chosen veg (see opposite) into the batter and make sure it's evenly coated. Allow any excess batter to drip off, then gently drop the veg into the oil. Fry until golden on one side and then turn over, using a slotted spoon (they will take around 1 minute 20 seconds on each side).

When the pakora is golden on both sides, lift it out of the oil and drain it on a piece of kitchen paper. Season with a generous pinch of salt on both sides. Repeat until all your veg is cooked. You can cook two or three pieces at the same time, depending on the size of your pan and the veg.

These pakoras are amazing with Date and Tamarind Chutney (page 215) or Green Chutney (page 221).

Autumn/winter veg

Cabbage, finely shredded

Brussels sprouts, finely shredded

Beetroot, grated raw, or cooked and sliced

Carrot, grated raw

Celeriac, grated raw

Butternut squash, roasted and sliced

Potatoes, boiled and sliced

Sweet potato, roasted and sliced

Cauliflower, cut into thin steaks (see page 18)

Kale, finely shredded

Leeks, thinly sliced

Onion, thinly sliced

Parsnips, grated raw, or roasted and sliced

Spring/summer veg

Broccoli, thinly sliced

Sprouting broccoli

Spinach, roughly shredded or whole leaves

Watercress, roughly shredded or whole leaves

Asparagus

Aubergine, thinly sliced

Peppers, thinly sliced

Fennel, thinly sliced

Runner beans

Samphire

Sorrel

Chard

New potatoes, boiled and sliced

Autumn/winter veg combos

Grated apple and beetroot

Grated pear and celeriac

Sweet potato and sliced spring onion

Kale and potato

Brussels sprout and beetroot

Cauliflower and leek

Spring/summer veg combos

Fennel and spinach

Sorrel and onion

Broccoli and watercress

Chard and red pepper

New potato and watercress

New potato and sorrel

ALOO TiKi

Aloo tiki are little fried potato cakes, served as street food snacks in India. I love the combination of fluffy potato and fresh peas with a crispy coating and a nice kick of pepper and cumin.

If you don't have semolina, you can swap it out for plain flour. I find the semolina adds a nice crispy texture.

Serves 4–6 as a starter/side

500g medium floury potatoes (such as King Edward or Maris Piper)

½ tsp ground turmeric

2 tbsp veg oil, plus extra to fry – at least 3 tablespoons

1 tsp black mustard seeds

1 tsp cumin seeds

1 medium red onion, finely chopped

4 garlic cloves, grated or crushed

A thumb-sized piece of ginger, grated

1 green chilli, finely chopped

100g frozen peas

A small bunch of coriander (stalks included), finely chopped

Juice of ½ lemon

1 tsp ground black pepper

1 tsp garam masala

4 tbsp semolina or plain flour

Salt

Put the potatoes, whole and unpeeled, into a large saucepan. Cover with cold water, and add the turmeric and at least 2 tablespoons of salt. Bring to the boil, then cook until they're nice and soft – it will take around 40 minutes from cold but will depend on the size and variety. Once the skin begins to crack, test if they're ready by poking them with a fork – it should slide very easily into the potatoes. Drain and leave to steam-dry in a colander.

While the potatoes are cooking, heat the oil in a frying pan on a medium heat and add the mustard and cumin seeds. When the seeds begin to pop, add the onion and the 1 teaspoon of salt and turn the heat down low to cook the onion really slowly. When the onion begins to soften – after about 5 minutes – add the garlic, ginger and green chilli, and cook until the onion is completely soft and caramelised (10–15 minutes in total). Then stir through the peas and take off the heat.

In a large bowl, mash the potatoes (no need to peel them) until smooth and add the onion and pea mixture. Stir in the coriander, lemon juice, black pepper, garam masala and 2 tablespoons of the semolina or flour. Mix well and taste for seasoning.

When the mixture has cooled, roll it into golf-ball-sized portions, then flatten them in between the palms of your hands into cakes. Put the remaining semolina or flour on a plate and press each of the flat sides of the tiki into it, so both sides are coated with semolina.

Coat the bottom of a frying pan with oil. Heat over a medium-high flame, then add the tiki (they should sizzle). Cook until golden brown (around 5 minutes), then carefully flip over and brown the other side.

Serve warm with Date and Tamarind Chutney (page 215) or Green Chutney (page 221). I also like to add a splash of colour with some Pink Onion Pickle (page 228).

BHEL PURi

Bhel puri is a form of chaat (see page 153), famous for being served as a late-night snack on the beaches of Mumbai (where I first encountered it). It's based around puffed rice, tangy tamarind chutney and fresh chopped veg.

Bhel puri must be eaten as soon as it's made, in order to get the perfect balance of crunchy, soggy, sweet and sour in one mouthful. If you leave it for anything more than a few minutes, it will all go soggy. If you're making this for lots of people, you can get everything prepped separately and mix it together at the last minute or, even better, get people to assemble their own bowls.

You can find unsweetened puffed rice in most supermarkets.

Serves 4 as a starter/side

2 small potatoes
70g puffed rice
100g peanuts (preferably red-skinned ones)
1 tsp ground cumin
1 tsp ground coriander
1 tsp smoked paprika
1 small tomato, deseeded and finely diced
¼ medium cucumber, deseeded and finely diced
½ medium red onion, finely diced
A small bunch of coriander (stalks included), finely chopped
Juice of ½ lemon
2½ tbsp Green Chutney (page 221)
2½ tbsp Date and Tamarind Chutney (page 215)
1 large poppadum
1 tbsp sev (optional), plus extra for garnish
Salt

Put the potatoes, whole and unpeeled, into a large saucepan. Cover with cold water and add at least 2 tablespoons of salt. Bring to the boil, then cook until they're nice and soft – it will take around 40 minutes from cold but will depend on the size and variety. Once the skin begins to crack, test if they're ready by poking them with a fork – it should slide very easily into the potatoes. Drain and leave to steam-dry in a colander. When they are cool enough to handle, cut into 1cm cubes.

Heat a large, dry frying pan on a low to medium heat and add the puffed rice. Toast until it turns a light brown and begins to smell toasty and delicious. Remove the rice into a large bowl and put the frying pan back on the heat. Add the peanuts and toast until they turn golden and begin to release their nutty aroma. Add them to the puffed rice. Add the potatoes, 1 teaspoon of salt, the ground cumin and coriander and the paprika to the rice and mix well.

Just before you serve the bhel puri, add the tomato, cucumber, onion, most of the coriander, the lemon juice and two chutneys, and mix quickly – you want to avoid it going soggy.

Transfer to a shallow bowl or plate and break the poppadum into small pieces over the top. Finish with the sev, if using, and a garnish of coriander.

PEA KACHORI

Kachori are pastry-encrusted balls of spiced peas. They are eaten as street food snacks in India and would make the perfect canapé for an Indian-inspired feast or party. They are best served with a chutney, as they can be a little dry by themselves. I thoroughly recommend pairing them with Coriander Chutney (page 213). They freeze really well so you can make them ahead of time, then cook as and when you want them.

Makes around 20 kachori

For the filling

600g frozen peas, defrosted
1 tbsp veg oil
1 tsp brown mustard seeds
2 tsp cumin seeds
1 tsp fennel seeds
4 large garlic cloves, grated
   or crushed
A thumb-sized piece of ginger,
   grated
2 fresh green chillies, finely
   chopped
1 tsp ground cinnamon
½ tsp chilli powder
1 tsp garam masala
1 tsp ground black pepper
½ tsp ground turmeric
1 tsp sugar
1½ tsp fine sea salt
Juice of ½ lemon

For the pastry

300g plain flour
½ tsp fine sea salt
1½ tbsp veg oil, plus extra
   for oiling
175ml hot water

Preheat the oven to 180°C.

Roughly mash the peas or pulse them in a blender until they're mashed but still have some texture.

Heat the oil in a large frying pan on a medium heat and add the mustard, cumin and fennel seeds. When they begin to pop, add the garlic, ginger and green chillies, followed by the peas, ground spices, sugar and salt. Stir-fry for 5 minutes until the spices are cooked and the smell of raw garlic has gone. Most of the moisture should have evaporated and the peas should still be bright green.

Take the pan off the heat and add the lemon juice. Transfer to a bowl.

To make the pastry, put the flour in a large bowl, make a well in the middle and add the salt and oil. Use your fingertips to rub the oil into the flour until it resembles fine breadcrumbs. Pour in two-thirds of the hot water, mix, then add the rest bit by bit, kneading it into the dough until it feels firm. Pour a drizzle of oil into your hands and rub them together. Pat the dough with your hands to keep it moist.

Separate the dough into 20 small balls (slightly smaller than a golf ball). When all your balls are prepped, use a rolling pin to roll them out on a clean, dry surface into circles, roughly 10cm in diameter and 1mm thick.

To make the kachori, put 2 teaspoonfuls of the pea mixture in the middle of a dough circle and bring the sides of the pastry up tightly around the peas so that it looks almost like a Chinese dim sum parcel. Seal the pastry at the top by twisting it tightly, then pinch off any excess pastry – otherwise you'll be left with a thick bunch of pastry at the top.

Press the kachori lightly between the palms of your hands to flatten it slightly from top to bottom and set aside. Continue until you have no dough left. The chances are they will get neater as you go but don't worry too much about uniformity.

Oil a baking tray and lay out the kachori pinched-side down – roll around so they become coated with the oil on all sides. Bake for 30 minutes or until golden brown, turning them over halfway through cooking.

Serve with Coriander Chutney (page 213).

TOFU TiKKA

When we used to go to our local curry house when I was a child (shout out to The Passage to India in Nailsworth!), I would always order Chicken Tikka. I have such clear memories of succulent chicken pieces, luminous pink with tandoori spice, lined up on a bed of sliced raw onion, with cooling raita and a wedge of lime on the side. Delicious! This is my plant-based tribute to that classic curry-house dish.

Serves 4 as a starter/side

500g good-quality, extra-firm tofu (I use Tofoo, which can be found in most supermarkets)
5 tbsp veg oil
1 green pepper, cut into 1cm chunks
1 red onion, ½ cut into 1cm dice, and ½ thinly sliced into half-moons to garnish
Coriander leaves, to garnish
1 lime, cut into 4 wedges, to garnish

For the marinade

220g plain unsweetened soya yoghurt (I use Alpro)
4 large garlic cloves, grated or crushed
A thumb-sized piece of ginger, grated
2 tsp smoked paprika
1 tsp hot chilli powder
½ tsp ground turmeric
2 tsp curry powder
½ tbsp ground cumin
½ tbsp ground coriander
1½ tsp salt
Juice of ½ lemon

Start by preparing the tofu. If it's in water, drain it and wrap it in kitchen paper or a clean tea towel. It's really important that the tofu is as dry as possible, so gently press down on it to encourage any excess water out. Cut it into 2cm cubes and set to one side on kitchen paper.

Mix the marinade ingredients in a bowl and add the tofu. Use your hands to evenly coat the tofu in the sauce. Marinate for 10 minutes–1 hour.

Heat 3 tablespoons of oil in a large frying pan on a high heat and wait for it to get smoking hot. Add the tofu and fry until one side of the tofu is golden brown. Turn over the tofu and repeat until all sides are browned. When the tofu is cooked, take it out of the pan and leave it to one side.

Heat 2 tablespoons of oil on a high heat in the same pan and add the green pepper and diced onion. When it's beginning to char, add the tofu back in and stir-fry for 30 seconds before taking the pan off the heat.

Place the tofu, peppers and onion on a plate and garnish with the sliced red onion and coriander. Serve with Coriander and Coconut Chutney (page 218) and lime wedges.

GOBi MANCHURiAN

This Indo-Chinese dish can be found on menus across India. I always seem to come across it in roadside service stations and restaurants when I'm travelling around. On a side note, I've had some seriously good meals in Indian service stations so if you find yourself in one, be sure to order some food.

Gobi Manchurian works well as a side dish or starter but it can also be served with rice or noodles as a main. The gobi – cauliflower – is traditionally deep-fried but I prefer to roast mine as I find the fried variety a bit too rich.

For the chilli sauce in the recipe, you can use pretty much whatever you have lying around at home – anything from sriracha to chilli table sauce will work. Remember that the spiciness will vary though – for example, if using sriracha, start with less.

Serves 4 as a starter/side

For the cauliflower
1 large cauliflower, cut into small
  florets
3 tbsp veg oil
1 tsp ground black pepper
1 tsp smoked paprika
½ tsp ground turmeric
1 tsp garam masala
½ tsp fine sea salt

Ingredients cont. page 170

Preheat your oven to 200°C.

Put the cauliflower in a large roasting tin. Pour the oil into a mug, add the ground spices and salt, and mix well. Pour the oil over the cauliflower, using your hands to make sure it's evenly coated with spiced oil. Roast for 25 minutes, or until the cauliflower is golden brown and beginning to char around the edges. You will need to stir the cauliflower halfway through cooking.

Recipe cont. page 170

For the sauce

3 tbsp veg oil

2 star anise

1 tsp cumin seeds

5 spring onions, thinly sliced
(save the green tops to garnish)

4 large garlic cloves, grated
or crushed

A thumb-sized piece of ginger,
grated

1 tsp smoked paprika

1 tsp chilli powder

1 tbsp chilli sauce
(see introduction)

2 tbsp light or dark soy sauce

3 tbsp ketchup

1 tbsp red wine vinegar

2 tsp sugar

1 tbsp cornflour

Salt

2 green chillies, chopped,
to garnish

Now make the sauce. Heat the oil in a large saucepan on a medium heat and add the star anise and cumin seeds. When they begin to turn golden, add the spring onions and turn the heat down low. When the onions begin to soften, add the garlic, ginger, paprika and chilli powder, along with a generous pinch of salt.

When the smell of raw garlic has gone (after around 3 minutes of frying), add the chilli sauce, soy sauce, ketchup, vinegar, sugar and cornflour. You must keep stirring the mix to avoid lumps forming. Slowly pour in 250ml water, stirring as you go. Simmer the sauce on a low heat for 5 minutes, allowing it to thicken. Taste for seasoning – you may need to add more salt.

Take the pan off the heat and stir through the roasted cauliflower so that it's evenly coated in the sauce. Garnish with the fresh green chilli and spring onion tops. If you find you have more sauce than is needed to coat the cauliflower, serve any extra in a small bowl as a dipping sauce. It will also make a delicious spicy chutney to serve with curry and rice.

SPICY NUTS

A few years ago, I spent Christmas with my parents in Kerala. We stayed in a tiny house by a deserted beach and had the most amazing hosts who would cook us the most delicious food every evening. Before dinner, when my dad cracked open the first Kingfisher of the night, we'd snack on 'kaju fry', a highly addictive mix of fried cashew nuts, curry leaves and chilli powder. These spicy nuts are my ode to those memorable festive Keralan evenings (see photo on page 238).

You can always leave the curry leaves out if you can't find fresh ones. These are best served warm and freshly cooked, but will last for up to a month stored in an airtight container.

Serves 6-8

100g almonds
100g pistachios
200g cashew nuts
100g pecans
1 tbsp veg oil
10 fresh curry leaves
1½ tsp hot chilli powder
1 tsp smoked paprika
1 tsp curry powder
½ tsp ground turmeric
1 tsp sugar
1½ tsp fine sea salt

Preheat the oven to 180°C.

Spread the almonds and pistachios out flat on a large baking tray and roast in the oven for 5 minutes. Take the tray out and add the cashews and pecans and roast for a further 5 minutes.

Heat the oil in a large frying pan on a medium heat and add the curry leaves. When they begin to crisp up, tip in the roasted nuts followed by the spices, sugar and salt. Turn down the heat and stir until the nuts are well coated with the spice mix. Take off the heat and transfer to a bowl to cool.

SPEEDY SAMOSAS

Nothing beats a proper traditional samosa but I appreciate that some of you don't have the time or patience to make your own from scratch. These samosas are for you lot. You probably have most of the ingredients lying around in your freezer and cupboards at home and, although many traditionalists will be tut-tutting at this method, I really do think they hit the spot nicely.

Microwave magic: As these are speedy samosas, feel free to use a microwave to cook the potatoes. Simply pierce them all over with a fork (no need to peel them) and microwave on full power for 5–10 minutes. Check they are well cooked all the way through by piercing them with a fork – it should slide very easily through them.

Makes roughly 22 samosas

2 tbsp veg oil, plus extra to brush the pastry
2 tsp brown mustard seeds
2 tsp cumin seeds
1 large white onion, finely diced
A thumb-sized piece of ginger, grated
2 green chillies, finely diced
3 medium potatoes, cooked (pages 27–9, or use microwave tip above)
300g diced frozen veg mix (such as carrots, sweetcorn and peas)
½ tsp ground turmeric
1 tsp ground black pepper
1 tsp garam masala
Juice of ½ lemon
2 × 270g packs of filo pastry
Nigella (black onion) seeds, to sprinkle on top
Salt

Preheat the oven to 200°C.

Heat the oil in a large frying pan on a medium heat. When it's hot, add the mustard and cumin seeds and fry until they turn golden and begin to pop. Add the onion and 1 teaspoon of salt, then turn the heat down low to cook the onion really slowly. When the onion starts to soften – about 5 minutes – add the ginger and green chillies, and cook until the onion is completely soft and caramelised (10–15 minutes in total).

While the onion is cooking, mash the potatoes.

When the onion is cooked, add the frozen veg, turmeric, black pepper and garam masala to the pan and stir until the veg has defrosted. Add the mashed potatoes to the pan with a large pinch of salt. Take the pan off the heat and stir through the lemon juice. Allow the mix to cool completely before moving to the next stage.

Carefully unroll a sheet of pastry onto a clean, flat surface (cover the rest of the pastry with clingfilm as you work to stop it drying out). Brush one side with oil and layer another sheet on top. Cut the sheets horizontally (widthways) into three even strips. Place a heaped teaspoon of the veg mix into the bottom right-hand corner of the strip and fold up over on itself to form a triangle. Fold it back down the other way to form another triangle and continue, working your way along the strip, encasing the mix in a pastry parcel. Brush the end with oil and stick it down to close.

Put the samosa on a baking tray and repeat this process until you've used all the pastry.

Brush the tops of the samosas lightly with oil and sprinkle over the nigella seeds.

Bake in the oven for 15 minutes or until light golden-brown. Serve with Tomato and Chilli Chutney (page 219).

SPiCED CRiSPY CHiCKPEAS

Warning – these chickpeas are totally addictive. I make them at least once a week for lunch, and often eat them simply sprinkled on top of a salad.

You can use them in the chaat salad on page 152 instead of the spiced chickpeas for a bit of extra crunch. We used to serve them on the street food stall on top of Kachumber Salad (page 233) and drizzled with Coriander Chutney (page 213). Don't be fooled by the simplicity, it's one of my favourite dishes that we've ever served!

Serves 4 as a snack/side

3 tbsp veg oil
1 × 400g tin of chickpeas, drained and rinsed
2 tsp ground cumin
1 tsp ground coriander
½ tsp ground cinnamon
1 tsp fine sea salt

Heat the oil in a large frying pan on a medium heat. When it's smoking hot, add the chickpeas and fry until they begin to crisp up and turn golden brown. This will take around 8 minutes – resist the temptation to stir them as they get crispier if you leave them alone. Around halfway through cooking, give the pan a shake.

When the chickpeas are golden, take the pan off the heat and add the ground spices. Shake the pan well to make sure they are evenly coated. Pour the chickpeas onto a plate lined with kitchen paper and then sprinkle them with the salt. Leave to cool for a minute or so before serving – this will help them get extra crispy. Serve with Kachumber Salad (page 233) and Coriander Chutney (page 213).

SIDES

When I'm in India, I rarely eat a single dish for a meal. I like to load my plate with a variety of smaller dishes so I can try as many different recipes and flavours as possible (time spent eating in India is extremely precious and must be maximised at every opportunity!). When I've had the privilege of eating in people's homes, I've found that this is also how Indians tend to eat when cooking for themselves. Regardless of how many people are around the table, dish upon dish is brought out accompanied by rice or roti, a sour pickle and usually a plate of raw red onion and a semicircle of lime.

I'm reluctant to use the term 'small plates' but this is the simplest way to describe this style of eating – small varied dishes that complement one another but stand as solo dishes in their own right too. That is how I view the dishes in this chapter. They are often ordered as accompaniments to curries, breads and rice in the curry house, but happily make up a meal on their own, too. The serving sizes stated are for serving the dishes as a side. But you can simply double the quantities for more substantial portions, or keep them small and make a few different dishes for the ultimate Indian feast.

JEERA ALOO

Whenever I eat home-cooked Indian food, I am always struck by how simple some of the dishes are. With just one or two spices and a pinch of salt, humble vegetables are elevated to new heights. Jeera translates as cumin and this is one of my favourite ways to eat potatoes – trust me on the amount of garlic …

Serves 4

3–4 medium floury potatoes (such as King Edward or Maris Piper)
4 tbsp veg oil
5 large garlic cloves, grated or crushed
1 tsp ground turmeric
1 tbsp cumin seeds
A large handful of coriander, roughly chopped (stalks included)
Salt

Fill a large saucepan with water and add at least 2 tablespoons of salt – it should taste as salty as the sea. Add the potatoes whole (don't peel them!) and bring to the boil. Cook until they are nice and soft – it will take around 40 minutes from cold but will depend on the size and variety. Once the skin begins to crack, test if they're ready by poking them with a fork – it should slide very easily into the potatoes. Drain and leave to steam-dry in a colander. When they are cool enough to handle, break them into 3cm chunks – don't worry if some pieces break up, these will turn deliciously crispy in the pan.

Heat the oil in a large frying pan on a high heat. When it's smoking hot, add the potatoes. They should begin to break up naturally, but you can always help them along with a wooden spatula. Leave them to crisp up on one side and then turn the heat down to medium and add the garlic, turmeric, cumin seeds and a generous pinch of salt. Give the whole lot a stir and leave for the other side to crisp up. When the garlic and spices are cooked through, take the pan off the heat and stir through the coriander. Taste for seasoning – potatoes love salt!

SPICED RED CABBAGE

We use red cabbage in the curry house as it's almost always in season and looks stunning on a loaded plate of curry and rice. This recipe is a spin on a red cabbage recipe my mum often cooks as part of a Sunday roast during the winter. I've added some chilli and earthy spices along with the classic red cabbage sidekicks, sugar and vinegar. This is the perfect warming winter dish and goes really well with a rich curry – it acts almost like a sweet and sour pickle.

Serves 4

2 tbsp veg oil
2 tsp cumin seeds
1 green chilli, slit lengthways
1 medium red onion, sliced into
    half-moons
1 medium red cabbage, thinly
    sliced
4 large garlic cloves, grated
    or crushed
½ thumb-sized piece of ginger,
    grated
4 tbsp red wine vinegar
1 tbsp sugar
1 tsp garam masala
Salt

Heat the oil in a large frying pan on a medium heat and add the cumin seeds and green chilli. When the seeds are golden and the chilli has begun to blister, add the onion along with a generous pinch of salt. Turn the heat down low and cook really slowly until the onion is completely soft and caramelised (10–15 minutes).

Add the cabbage, garlic and ginger, followed by the vinegar and sugar and another pinch of salt. Place a lid on top of your pan and cook the cabbage down for about 15 minutes – you want a mix of soft sweet pieces and crunchier bits for texture. Finish by stirring through the garam masala. Taste for seasoning.

BOMBAY POTATOES

Is there anything more comforting than crispy spiced potatoes with a fluffy middle? Bombay potatoes come in many forms – mine are garlicky, crispy and slightly spicy. They are heavenly and are an essential item on the menu of any self-respecting curry night.

Serves 4

3–4 medium floury potatoes (such as King Edward or Maris Piper)
90ml veg oil
3 tsp brown mustard seeds
4 large garlic cloves, grated or crushed
½ thumb-sized piece of ginger, grated or blitzed into a paste
2 tsp ground cumin
2 tsp ground coriander
1 tsp ground turmeric
1½ tsp hot chilli powder
A small bunch of coriander (stalks included), roughly chopped
Salt

Fill a large saucepan with water and add at least 2 tablespoons of salt – it should taste as salty as the sea. Add the potatoes whole (don't peel them!) and bring to the boil. Cook until they are nice and soft – it will take around 40 minutes from cold but will depend on the size and variety. Once the skin begins to crack, test if they're ready by poking them with a fork – it should slide very easily into the potatoes. Drain and leave to steam-dry in a colander. When they are cool enough to handle, roughly chop them – different sizes work well and make sure you keep all the smaller bits as these will turn deliciously crispy in the pan.

Heat a large frying pan on a high heat and add the oil. When it's smoking hot, add the mustard seeds. When they begin to pop, add the potatoes and a large pinch of salt. Resist the temptation to stir the potatoes as they need to crisp up on one side (this will take up to 5 minutes). When they have turned crisp and golden on one side, turn the potatoes over.

When they're starting to crisp up on the second side, add the garlic and ginger. Give the whole pan a good stir for a couple of minutes and add the rest of the spices. You can always add more oil if you need to, to stop the spices burning. You know the mix is cooked through when the smell of raw garlic has gone. Take the pan off the heat and stir through the chopped coriander. Taste for seasoning.

KERALAN GREEN BEAN THORAN

I first discovered thorans while travelling around Kerala as a teenager. Most meals would include a dish of vegetables sautéed with fresh coconut, curry leaves and mustard seeds. These aromatic stir-fries quickly became one of my favourite ways to cook vegetables and instantly transport me back to tropical Kerala, one of my favourite Indian states.

Fresh curry leaves really elevate this dish but if you don't have any to hand, it's fine to leave them out. This recipe is really versatile and you can swap the beans out for whatever veg you have lying around such as cabbage, cooked Brussels sprouts or Tenderstem broccoli.

Serves 4

1½ tbsp coconut oil
2 tsp brown mustard seeds
1 tsp cumin seeds
1 tsp fennel seeds
1 dried red chilli, ripped in half
10 fresh curry leaves (optional)
350g green beans, topped and
    cut in half
2 tsp sugar
A thumb-sized piece of ginger,
    grated
3 tbsp desiccated coconut
Juice of 1 lime
Salt

Heat 1 tablespoon of coconut oil in a large frying pan on a medium heat. Add the mustard seeds and fry until they pop. Add the cumin and fennel seeds, followed by the dried red chilli and curry leaves. Fry until they begin to crisp up, then take the pan off the heat.

Heat ½ tablespoon of coconut oil in another frying pan and add the beans, sugar and a pinch of salt. Stir through the ginger, adding a splash of water if needed. When the beans have begun to darken, add the coconut. Cook, stirring as you go, until the coconut begins to toast and the beans are cooked through – make sure you don't overcook the beans as they are best with a bit of bite in them. Stir through the fried spice mix and lime juice and take the pan off the heat. Taste for seasoning.

SAAG ALOO

Large-leaf spinach works best here – I find the stuff you get in a bag in the supermarket just wilts into oblivion. You'll find the more robust leaves in most greengrocers, farmers' markets or decent corner shops. If you don't have spinach to hand, rainbow chard or kale will work really well.

Serves 4

3 medium floury potatoes (such as King Edward or Maris Piper)
70ml veg oil
2 tsp brown mustard seeds
2 tsp cumin seeds
4 large garlic cloves, grated or crushed
½ thumb-sized piece of ginger, grated
2 tsp ground cumin
1 tsp ground coriander
½ tsp chilli powder
½ tsp ground turmeric
600g large-leaf spinach, washed and torn to pieces, tough stalks sliced
Juice of ½ lemon
Whole nutmeg, to season
Salt

Fill a large saucepan with water and add at least 2 tablespoons of salt – it should taste as salty as the sea. Add the potatoes whole (don't peel them!) and bring to the boil. Cook until they are nice and soft – it will take around 40 minutes from cold but will depend on the size and variety. Once the skin begins to crack, test if they're ready by poking them with a fork – it should slide very easily into the potatoes. Drain and leave to steam-dry in a colander.

Heat the oil in a large frying pan on a medium heat. When hot, add the mustard and cumin seeds, and fry until they begin to pop. Turn down the heat and add the garlic, ginger, cumin, coriander, chilli powder and ½ teaspoon of salt. You may need to add a splash of water to stop the spices from burning. Cook the spice mix until the smell of raw garlic has gone (around 5 minutes).

Roughly chop the potatoes and add them to the frying pan with a generous pinch of salt. Don't worry if some pieces break up – this gives the dish texture. Resist the temptation to stir, you want to leave the potatoes to colour (this will take around 5 minutes). When one side has turned golden, add the turmeric and stir. Add the torn spinach to the pan with a splash of water and another pinch of salt. You may need to add the spinach in stages, to fit it all in. Covering the pan with a lid will help the spinach wilt down more quickly. When the spinach has wilted into the potatoes, take the pan off the heat and add the lemon juice. Finish by grating over some nutmeg – about 7 grates should do it. Taste for seasoning – it may need a pinch of salt.

GUNPOWDER GREENS

'Gunpowder' is a popular spice mix in South Indian cooking, where it is known as molaga podi. It gets its name from the punchy quantity of dried chillies and the mix is ground to a similar consistency as gunpowder. This is a simplified version of the traditional mix and will make more than you need for the recipe. Stored in an airtight container, it will last at least a month and is a great way to spice up salads and stir-fries.

If you can't find the right dried red chillies, you can use chilli flakes.

Serves 4

70g sesame seeds
A large handful of dried red chillies
(ideally milder Kashmiri chillies
but if you can't find these, then
standard dried red chillies work,
just avoid the super-fiery small
Thai ones)
1 tsp sugar
30ml sesame oil
2 medium leeks, washed and
thinly sliced
1 small broccoli, cut into small
florets, stalks thinly sliced
150g kale, roughly shredded,
tough stalks removed
Juice of 1 lemon
A small bunch of coriander (stalks
included), roughly chopped
Salt

Start by making the gunpowder spice mix. Heat a medium frying pan on a medium heat and add the sesame seeds and dried red chillies. Toast until the seeds turn golden. Place in a spice grinder or blender with 1 teaspoon of salt and the sugar. Blitz to a rough powder.

Heat a large frying pan or wok on a medium heat and pour in the oil. When it's hot, add the leeks with a large pinch of salt, turn the heat down low and cook really slowly until they're soft (about 10 minutes).

Add the broccoli to the leeks, and when it begins to soften after a minute or two, add the kale. Cook until the kale has just started to wilt. Take it off the heat and add 2 tablespoons of the gunpowder mix. Finish by stirring through the lemon juice and coriander. Taste for seasoning.

ALOO GOBi

One of my favourite sides that we do at the curry house. The secret to a great aloo gobi is a generous amount of oil and soft vegetables.

Serves 4

3 small floury potatoes (such as King Edward or Maris Piper)
1 small cauliflower, cut into florets (keep the inner leaves)
100ml veg oil
2 tsp cumin seeds
A medium bunch of coriander (stalks included), roughly chopped
4 large garlic cloves, grated or crushed
½ thumb-sized piece of ginger, grated
2 tsp ground coriander
2 tsp ground cumin
2 tsp curry powder
1 tsp hot chilli powder
1 tsp ground turmeric
250g passata or chopped tomatoes
2 tsp sugar
Salt

Fill a large saucepan with water and add at least 2 tablespoons of salt – it should taste as salty as the sea. Add the potatoes whole (leave the skin on!) and bring to the boil. Cook until they are nice and soft – it will take around 40 minutes from cold but will depend on the size and variety. Once the skin begins to crack, test if they're ready by poking them with a fork – it should slide very easily into the potatoes. Drain and leave to steam-dry in a colander. When they are cool enough to handle, roughly chop them– don't worry if they fall apart into small pieces at this stage.

Next, cook the cauliflower florets (save the inner leaves) in exactly the same way as the potatoes. The cauliflower is cooked when a fork slides easily through it (after around 25–30 minutes) – the softer the cauliflower, the more flavour it will absorb. Leave it to steam-dry in a colander.

When all your veg is cooked, heat the oil in a large frying pan on a medium heat. Add the cumin seeds and three-quarters of the fresh coriander – watch out for spitting oil – and fry until the seeds are golden and the coriander has turned a darker shade of green (around 45 seconds). Add the garlic, ginger and cauliflower leaves you saved earlier. Stir-fry for a few minutes before adding the remaining spices, apart from the turmeric. Cook for 2 minutes, then add the potatoes and cauliflower to the pan and sprinkle over the turmeric along with a generous pinch of salt. Turn up the heat and stir, breaking up some of the larger pieces as you go. At this stage, you want to get some colour on the veg so fry until it begins to go golden brown in places. Add the passata or tomatoes and sugar and cook for 5 minutes. Take the pan off the heat and stir through the remaining fresh coriander. Taste for seasoning.

CABBAGE & FENNEL SABZi

'Sabzi' is a reasonably vague term used in Indian cooking to refer to vegetable dishes. I use it to refer to stir-fried veg dishes without a sauce (or 'gravy' as it is referred to in India). Cabbage is the perfect veg to stir-fry with spices – all varieties of cabbage work well but I particularly like the sweet crispness of a pointed cabbage.

The addition of fennel came about when my flatmate, Milla, walked into the kitchen while I was testing this recipe. She had bought a bulb of fennel and was worried it wouldn't be eaten, so I did the honourable thing and added it to my sabzi. It took the dish to a whole new level.

Serves 4

2 tbsp veg oil
2 tsp brown mustard seeds
2 tsp cumin seeds
1 green chilli, slit lengthways
1 medium white onion, sliced
  into half-moons
4 large garlic cloves, grated
  or crushed
A thumb-sized piece of ginger,
  grated
½ a large green cabbage, thinly
  sliced
1 small fennel, thinly sliced
½ tsp ground turmeric
1 tsp sugar
Juice of 1 lime
Salt

Heat the oil in a large frying pan on a medium heat and add all the seeds and the green chilli. When the seeds begin to pop and splutter, add the onion and 1 teaspoon of salt, and turn the heat down low to cook the onion really slowly. When the onion begins to soften – after about 5 minutes – add the garlic and ginger, and cook until the onion is completely soft and caramelised (10–15 minutes in total).

Add the cabbage, fennel, turmeric and sugar, along with a splash of water and turn the heat back up to medium. Stir until the turmeric has turned the veg an even golden yellow. Place a lid on the pan and cook for 15 minutes until the veg is soft. Take the pan off the heat and stir through the lime juice. Taste for seasoning.

BUiLD YOUR OWN SABZi

The chart below is designed to help you build your own sabzi recipes. Once you've mastered the art of a great sabzi, you'll be able to turn even the saddest of vegetables at the bottom of your fridge into quick, delicious weeknight dinners or sides for a curry feast.

Remember to season your sabzi with salt at both stage 2 and stage 4.

Serves 4
as a side

Stage 1:

Flavour 2 tbsp of oil with 1–3 of the spices below.

2 tsp cumin seeds

1 tsp fennel seeds

2 tsp brown mustard seeds

1 tsp coriander seeds

1 or 2 dried red chillies, ripped into quarters

10 fresh curry leaves

1 tsp ajwain seeds (also called lovage or carom seeds)

2 tsp nigella (black onion) seeds

1 tsp chilli flakes

Stage 2:

Add 1–3 of the ingredients below with a generous pinch of salt.

1 red onion, sliced into half-moons

1 white onion, sliced into half-moons

3 banana shallots, thinly sliced

4 large garlic cloves, peeled and grated

A thumb-sized piece of ginger, grated

1–2 green chillies, slit lengthways or sliced for extra heat

2 tbsp desiccated coconut

Stage 3:

When stage 2 is cooked, add 2 of the veg below.

2 large leeks, thinly sliced

2 handfuls of green beans, topped and cut in half

2 handfuls of sugar snap peas

2 handfuls of Tenderstem broccoli

2 handfuls of baby corn

1 roasted sweet potato, roughly diced

2 handfuls of frozen peas

2 handfuls of kale, roughly shredded

2 handfuls of spinach, roughly shredded

Stage 4:

When stage 3 is cooked, finish your sabzi with 1 or 2 of the ingredients below, with another pinch of salt.

Juice of 1 lemon

Juice of ½ lemon

Juice of 1 lime

Zest of ½ lime

1 tsp garam masala

2 tbsp desiccated coconut

1 tsp sugar (essential if you're cooking cabbage or green beans)

1 tsp ground turmeric

½ tsp ground black pepper

1 tbsp white wine vinegar

1 tbsp apple cider vinegar

CHANA ALOO

This dish can be served either as a side or a main. You can always add more tomatoes and stock if you want to thin it out to serve as a curry with rice.

Serves 4 as a side/2 as a main

70ml veg oil
1 tbsp cumin seeds
2 cloves
3 cardamom pods, crushed
1 bay leaf
1 dried red chilli
A small bunch of coriander (including stalks), roughly chopped (save a few leaves to garnish)
1½ medium red onions, sliced into half-moons (save the half to garnish)
4 large garlic cloves, grated or crushed
½ thumb-sized piece of ginger, grated
2 tbsp tomato purée
2 tsp sugar
4 large tomatoes, diced
2 medium floury potatoes (such as King Edward or Maris Piper), cut into 2.5cm chunks (skin on)
1 × 400g tin of chickpeas, drained and rinsed
300ml veg stock (page 32)
2 tsp garam masala
Salt

Heat the oil in a large frying pan on a medium heat. When it's hot, add the cumin seeds, cloves, cardamom and bay leaf, and fry until they turn golden and begin to release their delicious aromas.

Add the dried red chilli and most of the coriander (watch out for spitting oil) and fry until the leaves have turned a darker shade of green (around 45 seconds). Add the onion and 1 teaspoon of salt and turn the heat down low to cook the onion really slowly. When the onion begins to soften – after about 5 minutes – add the garlic and ginger, and cook until the onion is completely soft and caramelised (10–15 minutes in total).

Turn the heat up to medium and add the tomato purée and sugar, with a splash of water if needed. Cook for 2 minutes until the purée has turned a darker shade of red, then add the fresh tomatoes and fry until they begin to break down. Add the potatoes and chickpeas with a pinch of salt, stirring to coat them with the delicious onion spice mix. Pour in the veg stock, turn the heat up to bring the pan to a simmer, then let it cook on low for 20 minutes until the chickpeas and potatoes are soft and almost melting into the sauce.

Finish by stirring through the garam masala. Taste for seasoning. Spoon into a bowl and top with the saved sliced onion and leaves of coriander.

CURRY POWDER CAULI

Maybe I shouldn't admit it, but I love curry powder. Yes, of course, it isn't a substitute for the layering of flavours you get from mixing your own spices when cooking Indian food but I really do think there is a time and place for that comforting familiar smell and taste of golden yellow powder that has become so ubiquitous with British-Indian food. It also happens to be a match made in heaven with roasted cauliflower.

Serves 4

1 large cauliflower, cut into florets
   (keep the inner leaves)
90ml veg oil
1½ tbsp curry powder
1 tsp cumin seeds
1 tsp ground turmeric
Salt

Preheat the oven to 180°C.

Place the cauliflower florets and inner leaves into a large roasting tin and add the oil, spices and salt . Stir to coat the cauli evenly. Roast for 30 minutes or until it is soft and golden. Stir halfway through. Taste for seasoning and add more salt if needed when serving.

CRISPY TOFU 'PANEER'

Before going vegan, I loved paneer. The good news is that tofu makes a great substitute when cooked in a certain way. I often eat this dish straight up, but you can also add it to the tomato or coconut curry bases on pages 46–7 for a spin on a paneer curry.

It makes a great side as part of a curry feast.

Serves 4 as a side/2 as a main

For the crispy tofu

280g good-quality extra-firm tofu
  (I use Tofoo, which can be found
  in most supermarkets)
4 tbsp cornflour
1 tsp fine sea salt
1 tsp garam masala
½ tsp chilli powder
1 tsp ground cumin
1 tsp smoked paprika
½ tsp ground black pepper
1 tbsp nutritional yeast
3 tbsp veg oil

For the spiced onion mix

2 tbsp veg oil
2 tsp cumin seeds
1 medium red onion, sliced into
  half-moons
4 large garlic cloves, grated or
  crushed
A thumb-sized piece of ginger,
  grated
1 green chilli, slit lengthways
1 tbsp tomato purée
1 tsp sugar
½ tsp ground turmeric
125g frozen peas
Juice of 1 lemon, plus wedges
  to serve (optional)
Salt
A small bunch of coriander
  (stalks included), roughly
  chopped, to garnish

Start by preparing the tofu. If it's in water, drain it and wrap it in kitchen paper or a clean tea towel. Gently press down on it to encourage any excess water out. Set aside while you prepare the spiced coating.

Place the cornflour, salt and all the spices in a large bowl and sprinkle in the nutritional yeast, breaking up the flakes with your finger so they form a fine powder. Mix well.

Cut your tofu into 1.5cm cubes and coat them in the cornflour spice mix.

Put a large frying pan on a high heat and add the oil. When it's smoking hot, carefully add the tofu cubes, one by one, so that each piece has a side face down in the oil. Leave to fry on one side for a couple of minutes until it has turned crispy and golden and then turn the pieces over, so they crisp up on another side. Repeat until all sides are crispy and golden. Drain the tofu on a piece of kitchen paper on a plate and set to one side.

Now make the spiced onion mix. Heat the oil in a large frying pan on a medium heat. When it's hot, add the cumin seeds and fry until they turn golden brown. Then add the onion and 1 teaspoon of salt and turn the heat down low to cook the onion really slowly. When the onion starts to soften – after about 5 minutes – add the garlic, ginger and green chilli, and cook until the onion is completely soft and caramelised (10–15 minutes in total).

Add the tomato purée, sugar and turmeric, and cook for a few minutes – you may need to add a splash of water to stop the mix from burning. When the tomato purée has turned a darker shade of red, add the crispy tofu to the pan. Stir so that it is well coated with the spiced onion mix.

Turn up the heat and add the peas and lemon juice, and cook until the peas have just defrosted – you want to keep them a bit crunchy as it adds a lovely freshness. Remove the pan from the heat and taste for seasoning. Serve topped with chopped coriander and a fresh lemon wedge, if you like.

FRiED AUBERGiNE

I find aubergines one of the most luxurious vegetables to cook. When done right, they turn from squeaky and rubbery to silken, buttery morsels, which are the perfect carrier for spices and sauces. In order to do the aubergine justice, you need to give it a generous amount of oil and cook it down slowly. The Hindi name for this dish is Brinjal Bhaji. The word 'bhaji' can be translated as 'fried vegetable' which is essentially what this recipe is – mouth-watering fried aubergine in a gloriously thick spiced tomato sauce.

Serves 4

3 large aubergines, cut into large chunks
120ml veg oil
1 medium red onion, sliced into half-moons
4 large garlic cloves, grated or crushed
½ thumb-sized piece of ginger, grated
2 medium tomatoes, roughly chopped
A large pinch of dried fenugreek leaves
1 tsp chilli flakes
2 tsp ground cumin
2 tsp ground coriander
½ tsp ground turmeric
1 tbsp tomato purée
2 tsp sugar
A small bunch of coriander (stalks included), roughly chopped
1 tsp garam masala
Juice of ½ lemon
Salt

Place the aubergines on a baking sheet and sprinkle 1 tablespoon of salt over the exposed flesh. Set aside for 10 minutes. The salt will begin to draw the moisture out of the aubergines, allowing them to soften and therefore absorb more flavour in the pan.

Heat the oil in a large frying pan on a medium heat. When it's hot, add the onion with a large pinch of salt and turn the heat down low to cook the onion really slowly, until it is completely soft and caramelised (10-15 minutes). Turn up the heat to high and add the aubergines, garlic and ginger – fry for a few minutes until the aubergines are nice and brown on all sides.

Add the fresh tomatoes, fenugreek leaves and chilli flakes, and turn down the heat to medium. Fry for 5 minutes or so until the tomatoes begin to break down. Add the other spices, tomato purée and sugar. You may need to add a small splash of water at this point, but remember this is meant to be a dry dish so avoid making it too saucy.

Turn down the heat to low, place a lid on the pan and cook for around 10 minutes until the aubergines are starting to melt into the sauce and the oil has begun to separate from the tomatoes.

Take the pan off the heat and stir through the coriander, garam masala and lemon juice. Taste for seasoning.

TANDOORI CAULI STEAKS

I get asked a lot what my favourite vegetable is and every time, without hesitation, I say cauliflower. I just love how versatile it is – boiled in perfectly seasoned water it becomes soft and buttery; blitzed into a sauce it becomes silken and creamy; and roasted in an oven with a few simple spices it becomes smoky and meaty.

This recipe is a spin on one of the original SpiceBox recipes, our tandoori cauli steaks. When we started trading at street food markets in London in 2016, very few people had come across a cauliflower 'steak' but we soon built up a following of cauli-steak fanatics who couldn't get enough of our tender spiced slabs of cauliflower cooked over charcoal and served with our zingy Coriander Chutney (page 213 – the essential accompaniment).

If you have time to marinate the cauliflower in advance (overnight ideally), you can skip the oil and salt stage – just make the marinade, leave the cauliflower for 8–12 hours, then roast.

Serves 4 as a side/2 as a main

1 medium cauliflower, outer leaves removed and sliced into 1.5cm-thick steaks (see page 18)
3 tbsp veg oil (optional)
130g plain unsweetened soya yoghurt (I use Alpro)
4 large garlic cloves, grated or crushed
A thumb-sized piece of ginger, grated
1 tbsp smoked paprika
1 tsp chilli powder
½ tsp ground turmeric
1 tbsp curry powder
½ tbsp ground cumin
½ tbsp ground coriander
1 tsp fine sea salt
Juice of ½ lemon
Salt

Preheat your oven to 180°C.

If you're not marinating overnight, place the steaks in a roasting tin and cover with the oil and a generous pinch of salt, using your hands to make sure they are evenly coated. Set aside for 15 minutes until they have softened slightly.

Make the marinade by mixing together the yoghurt with the rest of the ingredients in a small bowl. Once the steaks have rested, spoon the yoghurt marinade over both sides of the steaks and again use your hands to make sure each side is well coated. Roast in the oven for 45 minutes–1 hour until the steaks are soft and golden brown. Check them after 20 minutes as they will need turning. Taste for seasoning. Serve with Coriander Chutney (page 213).

KERALAN BEETROOT THORAN

This recipe is based on a dish I ate in Kerala a few years ago. I had been suffering from a particularly nasty stomach bug and therefore hadn't eaten a proper meal for days. We arrived at our hosts' house on the stunning and serene backwaters and, when they offered to make us dinner, I leapt at the opportunity of a meal that wasn't a bowl of boiled rice water. The stand-out dish from that meal was a beetroot thoran. Thorans are traditional Keralan dishes made with vegetables (usually cabbage, green beans, carrots or bitter gourd) stir-fried with grated coconut, mustard seeds, curry leaves, chillies and turmeric. I had eaten many thorans during my time in Kerala but never one made with beetroot – it worked perfectly. It is also a stunning dish visually, due to the bright white coconut against the pinky red of the beetroot with flashes of crispy green curry leaves.

I've suggested pre-cooked beetroot here as it's the easiest to work with but this would work just as well with grated raw beetroot or any variety of roasted beetroot (just make sure you give yourself enough time to cook it through, it usually takes at least an hour at 180°C, wrapped in foil).

Serves 4

3 tbsp coconut or veg oil
2 tsp brown mustard seeds
1 tsp cumin seeds
1 green chilli, slit lengthways
½ tsp chilli flakes
10 fresh curry leaves (optional, leave out if you can't find fresh)
1 medium red onion, sliced into half-moons
A large thumb-sized piece of ginger, grated
5 tbsp desiccated coconut
4 medium cooked beetroot, thinly sliced into half-moons
½ tsp ground turmeric
Juice of ½ lemon
Salt

Heat the oil in a large frying pan on a medium heat and add the mustard and cumin seeds. Fry until they begin to pop, then add the green chilli, chilli flakes and curry leaves. Fry for a minute until the green chilli starts to blister and the curry leaves crisp up, then add the onion and 1 teaspoon of salt. Turn the heat down low to cook the onion really slowly. When the onion begins to soften – after about 5 minutes – add the ginger, and cook until the onion is completely soft and caramelised (10–15 minutes in total).

When the onion is cooked, turn the heat up to medium and add 4 tablespoons of coconut. Once it starts to turn golden brown, add the beetroot and turmeric and stir well. When the beetroot is warmed through, take the pan off the heat and add the lemon juice. Taste for seasoning. Garnish with the remaining tablespoon of coconut.

PICKLES & CHUTNEYS

If you've got this far, you're well on your way to mastering the basics of cooking amazing Indian food. So now it's time to take things to the next level. In my opinion, an Indian meal can never reach its true potential without the tangy sharp kick of a pickle or a sweet spoonful of chutney. Or, even better, the heavenly contrast of both on the same plate.

The idea of pickling or whipping up a homemade chutney can be daunting to most home cooks but it's way easier than you think. And, once you've mastered the building blocks of both, you're able to pick and choose which fruit and veg you want to preserve in your choice of vinegar or sugar.

In this chapter, I've tried to stick mainly to fruit and veg you can easily find in UK shops – no green mangoes here! Pickling and chutney-making come into their own when you find yourself with an abundance of seasonal produce, so next time you come across a pile of bruised apples or a bunch of softening radishes in the bottom of your fridge, you know what to do.

A NOTE ON STERILISING JARS

Sterilising your jars before you put pickles and chutneys in them reduces the risks of bacteria forming and ensures that your preserves will last as long as possible. The easiest way to do this is by first washing your jars and lids separately in hot soapy water. When they're clean but still wet, place them on a baking tray and into a warm oven, set to 150°C, for 10 minutes. Leave to cool before decanting your chutney or pickle.

CORIANDER CHUTNEY

If I had a signature recipe, this would be it! This coriander chutney is a hybrid of a classic Indian coriander chutney and an Argentinian chimichurri. It is super-punchy in flavour and highly addictive – it goes with almost anything but is particularly special drizzled over Tandoori Cauli Steaks (page 204) and roast vegetables. In my opinion, a summer BBQ isn't complete without a bowl of this bright green sauce to slather over everything in sight.

Makes c.1 kg

100ml veg oil
5 garlic cloves
2 green chillies, stems removed
2 tsp salt
2 tsp sugar
Juice of 2 limes
3 tbsp white wine vinegar
3 large bunches of coriander, stalks included
A small bunch of flat-leaf parsley, stalks included

Put all the ingredients in a blender with 100ml water and blitz until a smooth chutney is formed. If you have a small blender, start by blending everything apart from the herbs, then slowly add the herbs in bit by bit. Decant into a container and keep in the fridge. It will last up to 7 days but is best eaten fresh.

SPiCED APPLE CHUTNEY

This is a great chutney to make in autumn when there is a glut of many different varieties of apples. I have put cooking apples in the ingredients as they cook down best, but you can also mix it up with whatever apples you have to hand – just remember that they take different times to cook down, and they have varying levels of sweetness.

I find that this chutney makes a great replacement for mango chutney with curries – it has the same sweet-sour balance of flavour.

Makes c.1kg

1 tbsp coriander seeds
1 cassia bark or cinnamon stick
6 cloves
2 medium white onions, roughly
    chopped
1kg cooking apples, cored and
    roughly chopped (skin on)
A thumb-sized piece of ginger,
    grated
1 tbsp chilli powder
1 tbsp garam masala
340g granulated sugar
425ml malt vinegar

Heat a large saucepan on a medium heat and add the whole spices. Toast until they turn golden and start to smell aromatic. Add all the other ingredients and slowly bring to the boil until the sugar has dissolved.

Simmer for 2 hours, stirring from time to time to stop the chutney sticking to the pan.

Pour the chutney into sterilised glass jars and seal immediately while still hot.

The chutney will last up to 2 months stored in a cool, dark cupboard. Once opened, store in the fridge.

DATE & TAMARiND CHUTNEY

This is the first chutney recipe I ever made. It's so simple yet has such an amazing layering of flavour to it – the sweetness of the dates perfectly offset by the tanginess of the tamarind, and the whole thing is wrapped up with the warmth of the garam masala. This is our signature chutney at SpiceBox – we've even been known to sell a bottle or two to guests who can't get enough of it.

Makes c.1 kg

250g pitted dates
175g tamarind paste
2 tsp garam masala

Put the dates into a large saucepan and add 400ml water. Bring to the boil, then add the tamarind and garam masala and simmer for 5 minutes. Take off the heat and leave to cool. Put it into a blender or food processor and blitz until smooth. Store in sterilised jars and keep in the fridge. This chutney will last at least 4 weeks.

CORiANDER & COCONUT CHUTNEY

This is a fresher, herbier version of the Coconut Chutney (page 220) and is amazing served with summer BBQs or super-spicy curries.

Makes c.170g

2 tsp cumin seeds
100g desiccated coconut
100ml coconut milk
1 green chilli, stem removed
A small bunch of coriander (stalks included), roughly chopped
A thumb-sized piece of ginger, roughly chopped
2 tsp fine sea salt
1 tsp sugar
Juice of 1 lime

Heat a small frying pan on a medium heat. Add the cumin seeds and toast until golden.

Add all of the ingredients to a blender and blitz until smooth. Taste for seasoning.

This will last at least a week stored in the fridge.

TOMATO & CHILLI CHUTNEY

Enjoy this chutney as a spicy alternative to tomato ketchup.

Makes c.500g

150ml veg oil
2 tsp cumin seeds
2 tsp brown mustard seeds
1 large white onion, roughly
   chopped
1 tsp fine sea salt
8 garlic cloves
A thumb-sized piece of ginger,
   roughly chopped
4 green chillies, stems removed
1 tsp ground turmeric
1 tbsp chilli flakes
2 tsp ground coriander
2 tsp ground cumin
1 tsp ground black pepper
½ tsp ground cinnamon
1 tsp chilli powder
1 tsp garam masala
2 tbsp tomato purée
2 tbsp sugar
1 × 400g tin of chopped tomatoes
3 tbsp white vinegar

Heat the oil in a large saucepan on a medium heat. Add the cumin and mustard seeds and fry until they start to pop. Add the onion, salt, garlic, ginger and green chillies, turn the heat down low and fry for 10 minutes until the onion has softened and the small of raw garlic has gone. Add the rest of the ground spices, the tomato purée and the sugar, and cook for 5 minutes.

Once the spice paste is cooked, add the chopped tomatoes and vinegar, and simmer for 5 minutes.

Take the pan off the heat and leave to cool. Transfer to a blender and blitz into a smooth sauce.

Pour into sterilised jars and keep in the fridge. This will last a couple of months unopened. Once open, eat within 3 weeks.

COCONUT CHUTNEY

One of my absolute favourite Indian dishes is masala dosa – I'd eat it every day if I could. Dosas are thin crispy pancakes made with fermented rice and lentil flour and are served with tomato and coconut chutneys. This chutney recipe is based on the coconut chutney I eat with dosa and is served at SpiceBox alongside our own take on the dosa – dosa waffles (or doffles as we affectionately refer to them).

I recommend eating this chutney with Bombay Potatoes (page 184) or the 15–Minute One–Pot Dhal on page 118.

Makes c.170g

2 tbsp veg oil
2 tsp brown mustard seeds
1 tsp cumin seeds
2 dried red chillies, ripped into quarters
10 fresh curry leaves (optional)
100g desiccated coconut
100ml coconut milk
A thumb-sized piece of ginger, roughly chopped
1 green chilli, roughly chopped
Juice of 1 lemon
1 tsp fine sea salt
1 tsp sugar

Heat the oil in a frying pan on a medium heat and add the mustard and cumin seeds. Fry until they begin to pop, then add the dried red chillies and curry leaves and fry until they crisp up. Take the pan off the heat.

Put the rest of the ingredients in a blender and top up with 200ml water. Blitz until smooth. Pour the chutney into a bowl and stir through the fried spice mix.

You can store the chutney in a jar in the fridge and it will last at least a week.

GREEN CHUTNEY

This classic Indian chutney may be familiar to you from the chutney tray served with poppadums in most British curry houses. It's super-fresh and works really well alongside richer curries.

Makes c.240g

A large bunch of mint (leaves only), roughly chopped
A large bunch of coriander (stalks included), roughly chopped
2 green chillies, stems removed
A thumb-sized piece of ginger, roughly chopped
1 tsp ground cumin
Juice of 1 lemon
1 tsp fine sea salt

Put all the ingredients in a blender along with 3 tablespoons of water and blitz until smooth. Taste for seasoning – you may need to add a touch more lemon and/or salt. Decant into a container and keep in the fridge. It will last up to 7 days but is best eaten fresh.

MANGO & APRICOT CHUTNEY

This is my take on a homemade mango chutney. Finding enough ripe mangoes to make mango chutney in the UK can be difficult and expensive – not to mention the food miles involved. I've created this recipe with ingredients you may well have lying around your store cupboards, or can easily find in the supermarket all year round.

Makes c.500g

500g tinned mango pulp
250ml white wine vinegar
2 garlic cloves, grated
A thumb-sized piece of ginger, grated
300g dried apricots, finely diced
1 tsp cumin seeds
1 tsp coriander seeds
5 cardamom pods, seeds removed and husks discarded
½ tsp chilli powder
2 tsp nigella (black onion) seeds
1 tsp fine sea salt
Juice of 1 lemon

Add the mango pulp, vinegar, garlic and ginger to a large saucepan and bring to the boil. Turn the heat down and simmer until the mixture reduces by a couple of centimetres (around 30 minutes), then add the dried apricots.

While the chutney is simmering, heat a frying pan on a medium heat and add the cumin, coriander and cardamom seeds. Toast until they're golden and aromatic and transfer to a pestle and mortar or small blender. Crush the seeds to a powder and then add them to the saucepan, followed by the chilli powder, nigella seeds and salt.

When the chutney has reduced and has a thick syrupy consistency, take the pan off the heat and add the lemon juice.

Pour the hot chutney into sterilised glass jars and seal immediately while still hot. The chutney will last up to 3 months stored in a cool, dark cupboard. Once opened, store in the fridge and eat within a month.

PRESERVED LEMON PiCKLE

Preserved lemons aren't traditionally Indian, but I find they make a great alternative to the classic curry sidekick of lime pickle, which is prepared in a very similar way to preserved lemons. Lemons are cheaper than limes and go further so I prefer to use them when cooking at home.

Don't be intimidated by the concept of preserving lemons, it's actually very easy. They are such a good ingredient to have at home and can be added to curries and stews for an extra flavour kick.

Fills a large 1.8-litre-Kilner jar

8 unwaxed lemons, well scrubbed
8 tbsp good-quality sea salt
(I use Maldon)
1 tbsp coriander seeds
1 tbsp black peppercorns
2 green chillies, slit lengthways

Take a lemon and cut the knobbly bits off each end. Stand it upright and slice it down the middle three-quarters of the way to the bottom (so you keep the lemon intact). Turn the lemon 90 degrees and repeat so that you've made a cross shape in the lemon and it opens up like a flower. Open the lemon and place a tablespoon of salt in the middle. Close the lemon and place in a wide-mouthed sterilised glass jar.

Repeat this process, squishing the lemons down so they are tightly compacted in the jar and releasing their juice. Once all the lemons are in the jar there should be enough lemon juice in the jar to completely cover them. If not, try squishing them down more with a pickle packer or rolling pin. You can always top up with more lemon juice if they're not covered.

Now add the spices and the chillies and fasten the lid. Give the jar a good shake, making sure the lemons remain fully submerged in the juice. Leave to ferment for 3–4 weeks in a cool, dark place. The lemons are ready when they've completely softened. Once opened, keep in the fridge for up to 6 weeks.

GUJURATi CARROT PiCKLE

I first tried this carrot pickle when Alpesh (who I run SpiceBox with) gave me a huge jar of his mum's to keep in my fridge. It's such a great accompaniment to curry as it adds crunch, zing and spicy heat. This is a really simple pickle to make and is a great intro to pickling for newbies.

Split yellow mustard seeds can be found in most Indian supermarkets. You can also order them online. Thank you to Mrs Chauhan for introducing me to carrot pickle and thank you for all the delicious packed lunches over the years.

Makes c.1kg

8 medium carrots, peeled and cut
   into 2.5cm-long, thin batons
1 tsp fine sea salt
½ tsp ground turmeric
2 tbsp veg oil
Juice of 1 lemon
3 tbsp split yellow mustard seeds
4 green chillies, slit lengthways
500ml malt vinegar

Put the carrots sticks in a large mixing bowl, add the salt and turmeric, and stir well. Leave for an hour – the salt will draw out some of the moisture from the carrots. Add the oil, lemon juice, mustard seeds, green chillies and vinegar, and mix well.

Transfer the pickle to a sterilised jar and put in the fridge. It will be ready after 12 hours and will last at least a month.

GARLIC PICKLE

Ever since I wrote this recipe for the book, I've had a jar of this in my fridge. When Alpesh tried it, he said it was his favourite pickle of mine. It is delicious served with dhal and roti. It also works very well with some vegan cheese and crackers.

Top tip for quickly peeling lots of garlic: put the cloves in a large jar with a lid or a cocktail shaker and shake vigorously for 30 seconds. Just like magic, the skins will separate from the cloves.

Makes c.170g

1 tsp fenugreek seeds
2 tsp brown mustard seeds
150ml veg oil
30 garlic cloves, cut in half lengthways
½ tsp fine sea salt
2 tsp chilli flakes
½ tsp ground turmeric
½ tsp sugar
Juice of 1 lemon

Heat a dry frying pan on a medium heat and toast the fenugreek and mustard seeds until golden and aromatic. Grind to a fine powder in a blender or pestle and mortar. Set to one side.

Heat the oil in a large frying pan on a medium heat and add the garlic and salt. Turn the heat down low and fry until the garlic is a dark golden brown (around 15 minutes). Add the chilli flakes, turmeric, ground fenugreek and mustard seeds, and sugar. Fry for a minute, then take the pan off the heat and add the lemon juice.

Put the mixture in a sterilised jar and store in a cool, dark place. It will be ready to eat after 12 hours but will last a couple of months stored like this. Refrigerate once opened and eat within 3 weeks.

PiNK ONiON PiCKLE

This sweet, sour, salty, bright pink pickle is a SpiceBox icon. It can be found adorning most of our dishes in the curry house. It is unbelievably simple to make and can be used to jazz up anything from simple dhals to salads. I always have a bowl of it in my fridge – and you should too!

Serves 4–6 as a garnish

1 large red onion, thinly sliced
    into half-moons
½ tsp fine sea salt
Juice of 1 lime

Put the onion in a small bowl and add the salt. Massage the salt into the onion and leave to one side for 20 minutes. In this time, the salt will draw the moisture out of the onion and it will go soft and translucent.

Add the lime juice and massage it in. Leave for an hour until the lime juice has turned the onion bright pink.

This pickle will keep in the fridge for 2 weeks.

GREEN CHiLLi PiCKLE

If you're a fan of heat, then this pickle is a great one to have in your fridge to spice up mealtimes.

Makes c.280g

150g green Indian chillies, washed, stems removed and cut in half lengthways
2 tsp fine sea salt
2 tsp split yellow mustard seeds
2 tsp veg oil
Juice of 3 lemons
2 tbsp malt vinegar
1 tsp ground turmeric
2 tsp sugar

Place the chillies in a bowl and add the rest of the ingredients. Mix so that the chillies are well coated with the other ingredients. Wash your hands well after handling the chillies.

Put the pickle into a sterilised glass jar and store in a cool, dark cupboard for up to 3 months. It will be ready to eat after 12 hours. Refrigerate once opened and eat within 3 weeks.

CABBAGE & FENNEL PiCKLE

I love the combination of cabbage and fennel. This fresh crunchy pickle is great with curries, but I also mix it into salads for added zing and texture.

Makes c.1kg

500g green cabbage, finely shredded
1 fennel bulb, finely shredded
2 tbsp fine sea salt
550ml apple cider vinegar
400g granulated sugar
2 tsp brown mustard seeds
1 tsp fennel seeds
1 tsp black peppercorns
Juice of 2 lemons

Place the cabbage and fennel in a large bowl and cover them with the salt. Massage the salt into the veg until well incorporated and then set aside for 1 hour. The salt will draw out some moisture from the cabbage and fennel.

Put the vinegar, sugar, mustard seeds, fennel seeds and peppercorns in a saucepan and bring to the boil. Turn the heat down and simmer for 20 minutes until the liquid has reduced. Set to one side for 10 minutes to allow the spices to infuse the liquid.

Place the cabbage mix into sterilised jars and pour over the pickling liquid and lemon juice. Once the mixture is at room temperature, seal and leave for at least 12 hours to pickle. This will keep in the fridge for at least a month.

SPRiNG RADiSH PiCKLE

This is a great way to preserve beautiful pink radishes when they come into season at the start of summer, but the recipe would work just as well with any radish variety.

Makes c.500g

250g pink spring radishes, thinly
   sliced
1 tbsp fine sea salt
3 tbsp veg oil
2 tsp brown mustard seeds
1 tsp fenugreek seeds
2 green chillies, slit lengthways
½ tsp ground turmeric
3 tbsp white wine vinegar
1 tbsp granulated sugar
Juice of 2 limes

Put the radishes in a large bowl and massage in the salt. Set aside for 10 minutes.

Meanwhile, heat the oil in a frying pan on a medium heat and add the mustard and fenugreek seeds and the green chillies. When they begin to pop and turn golden, add the turmeric and fry for a minute.

Add the vinegar and sugar and stir until the sugar dissolves. Take the pan off the heat and add the liquid to the radishes. Finish by adding the lime juice.

Once it's at room temperature, transfer to a sterilised glass jar. The pickle will be ready to eat after 12 hours and will last at least a month stored in the fridge.

RAITA

Every curry night needs a pot of cooling creamy raita. Silken tofu makes for a great yoghurt replacement – it has a really neutral flavour and goes super-creamy when whizzed up in a blender.

Makes c.500g

1 × 340g pack of silken tofu, drained
½ cucumber, roughly chopped
A small bunch of mint (leaves only)
½ tsp ground cumin
½ tsp ground black pepper
½ tsp fine sea salt
Juice of 1 lemon

Put all the ingredients into a blender or food processor and blitz until a smooth sauce is formed. Taste for seasoning – it may need a touch more lemon or salt. Store in the fridge and eat within 5 days.

KACHUMBER SALAD

You'll know this classic Indian chopped salad from the pickle and chutney trays that are served with the poppadums in most curry houses. My mum never serves a curry without a side of kachumber – it adds such a great freshness to your plate and a good contrast of texture to a saucy curry. Of course, it is delicious served on top of poppadums too.

Serves 4

2 medium tomatoes, finely diced
1 medium cucumber, deseeded and finely diced
½ medium red onion, finely diced
A small bunch of mint (leaves only), finely chopped
A small bunch of coriander (stalks included), finely chopped
½ tsp fine sea salt
½ tsp sugar
¼ tsp ground black pepper
Juice of 1 lime

Place everything in a bowl and mix well. Serve straight away.

RED ONION SALAD

This is perhaps one of the simplest recipes in the book but I wanted to include it as I can't eat a curry or dhal without a sidekick of red onion salad. I was introduced to the delights of the red onion salad on my first trip to India – at almost every place I'd eat, from roadside shacks to fancy Delhi restaurants, a dhal or curry would always be accompanied with a small bowl of sweet yet astringent slices of red onion, lime and green chilli. These ingredients provide a perfect trinity of flavours and textures that really bring out the best of Indian cooking. The raw chillies are for the spice lovers round the table, while the lime can help to soften the blow.

Serves 4 as a side

1 large red onion, thinly sliced into
    half-moons
1 lime, sliced into 4 wedges
2 green chillies, slit lengthways

Assemble all the ingredients on a small plate and place on the table for people to help themselves.

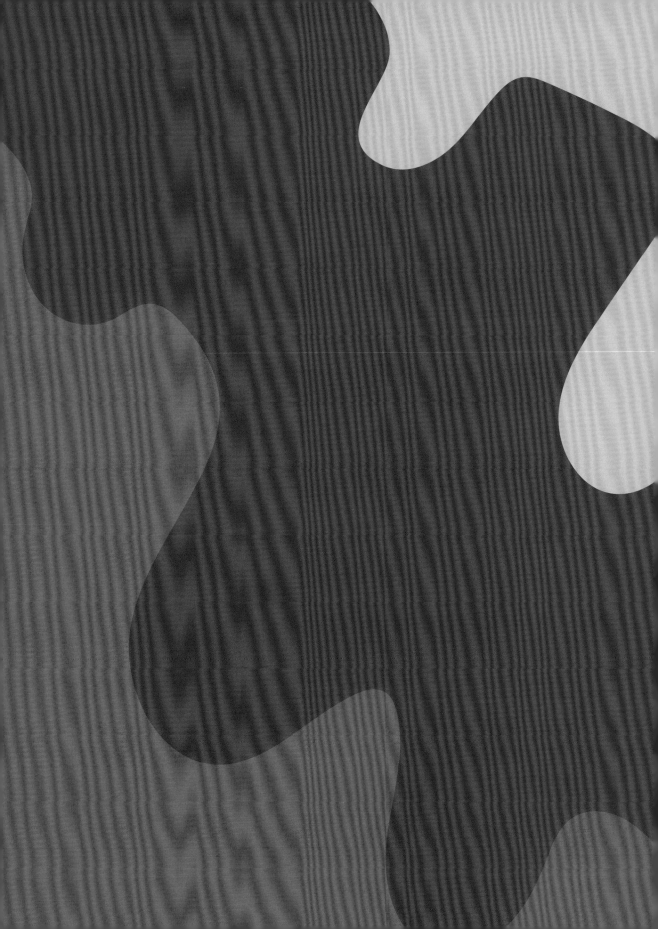

DRINKS

Indian cuisine is not famous for its desserts, and after a full-on Indian feast I rarely have room for pudding. However, I am partial to a creamy, thick mango lassi to satisfy my sweet tooth or a warming masala chai to help me digest. Moreover, on a steamy hot summer's day in Delhi, nothing beats stopping for a salty lime soda to help quench my thirst and rehydrate me.

If you have a go at making these recipes, you may find you'll never be able to drink lemonade again without adding a pinch of salt, or that bedtime is not complete without a warm mug of golden milk to settle your senses.

GOLDEN MiLK

Turmeric milk has been drunk for centuries in India but has only recently become well known in the West, thanks to a plethora of trendy cafés serving up turmeric lattes for the wellness tribe.

I love drinking this on a cold winter's evening before bed.

You will notice that I've totally contradicted myself in this recipe and asked you to peel the ginger. This is because the skin will leave little bits in the milk which are totally harmless but not ideal if you're after a smooth drink.

Serves 2

½ tsp ground turmeric or
1½ tsp grated fresh turmeric
½ tsp ground cinnamon
¼ tsp ground black pepper
A small thumb-sized piece of
ginger, peeled and grated
2 mugs of plant milk (I use oat
milk)
2 tsp maple syrup, agave syrup
or brown sugar

Put the spices in a mug and add a dash of the milk. Use a teaspoon to mix the spices into a smooth paste, then top up the mug with milk, give everything a good stir and pour the mix into a saucepan. Add the remaining ingredients and bring to a gentle boil, then simmer for 5 minutes. Pour into two mugs and serve.

MASALA CHAI

If you've ever visited India, you'll know how many cups of this sweet milky tea are consumed a day across the country. I love sipping on a sweet chai after a meal or with breakfast on a cold winter's morning.

Serves 2

½ thumb-sized piece of ginger
1 cassia bark or cinnamon stick
4 cardamom pods, crushed
1 bay leaf
2 cloves
¼ tsp ground black pepper
2 mugs of plant milk (I use oat)
2 black teabags
2 tsp sugar

Take the ginger and give it a good bash with a rolling pin so that the juices are released from it.

Put all the ingredients in a saucepan, bring to a gentle boil, then simmer for 5 minutes until the tea is infused with the spices.

Taste for sweetness – you may want to add more sugar if you like your tea sweet. Strain before serving.

MANGO LASSI

People go crazy for the mango lassi we serve at the curry house. We have one guest who comes in most nights with an empty flask, just to fill it up with a takeaway lassi.

Serves 2

400ml coconut drink (I use Alpro)
4 tbsp soya yoghurt
4 tbsp tinned mango pulp
Juice of ½ lime
¼ tsp fine sea salt

Place all the ingredients in a blender or jug and blitz or whisk until smooth. Store in the fridge and serve well chilled.

SPICED INDIAN LEMONADE

Also known as Nimbu Pani, this is the ultimate refreshing drink on a hot summer's day. The salt helps with rehydration and brings out the flavours of the spices.

Serves 2

2 sprigs of mint
Juice of 1½ limes
¼ tsp black salt (also sold as kala namak, but you can use regular sea salt if you can't find it)
A tiny pinch of ground black pepper
⅛ tsp ground cumin
1 tbsp sugar
A handful of ice

Put the mint sprigs in a pestle and mortar and give them a good bash to help release their flavour. If you don't have a pestle and mortar, you can just bash them with a rolling pin. Put them in a jug, along with the other ingredients and 600ml water, and mix well.

Taste for seasoning – you may want to add a touch more lime, salt, cumin or sugar.

SALTY-SWEET LIME SODA

I drink this relentlessly when I'm in India – I find it so hydrating and refreshing.

Serves 2

Juice of 2 limes
600ml sparkling or soda water
¼ tsp fine sea salt
2 tsp sugar
A handful of ice

Put all the ingredients into a jug and mix well.

Taste for seasoning – you may want to add a touch more lime, salt or sugar.

THANK YOU

I'd like to start by thanking Alpesh for agreeing to help me build my dream and sticking by me ever since. Business relationships are never easy and, despite our ups and downs, I count myself lucky every day that I ended up sharing a kitchen with you and that you ended up sharing your knowledge with me. Thank you for your relentless drive, awe-inspiring work ethic, meticulous attention to detail, refreshing (and sometimes bruising) honesty and introducing me to the Costa coconut flat white. Finally, thank you for believing in me.

Thank you to everyone who ever helped me during the early days of SpiceBox – when you start a business you have to pull in *a lot* of favours, and I was extremely lucky to be surrounded by such generous people. Firstly, thanks to Sagar for keeping me sane in Silicon Valley and for agreeing to move back to London and start SpiceBox with me. Thanks to Jess Deacon for grafting, cooking and gazebo erecting when I was a one-woman band. Thanks to Stella and Marina for all your hard work and loyalty. Thanks to Linh, George, Bert, Ernie, Max, Jack, Gonzalo, Holly, Jason and everyone else who worked on the street food stall over those crazy summers and gruelling winters. Thanks to Rupal for all the cooking, Charlie May for the events planning, Bethan and Joe for the number crunching, Lucy for the photo taking, Alice and Faraz for the designing, Adam Biddle for the connecting, David Haimes for the advising. Thanks to Sareta Puri for all of your help over the first few years. Thanks to James Otton for being the longest-serving member of the SpiceBox team. Thanks to Lawrence for putting up with me when I came home cold, wet and miserable, for unloading and re-loading the van on your days off, for being roped in to work on the stall for free.

Thanks to Sandor and John for your belief and support. I am incredibly fortunate to have you on board with this journey.

Thank you to everyone who helped put this book together. Thanks to my agent Cathryn Summerhayes for taking a punt on me and my editors Celia and Vicky for making this all happen during a global pandemic. Thanks to Clare for humouring my strange colour-combo requests and helping to make this book look sexy. Thanks to the *incredible* team who helped turn my recipes into art – Rosie Ramsden, Joff Lee, Rosie French, James Lee and Tabitha Hawkins. Those ten days on set were some of the most enjoyable days of work I've had. Thank you also for your constant words of support about my food, they mean a lot to me.

Thank you *so* much to all the recipe testers who generously gave up their time to cook my recipes and give me invaluable feedback: Alex Bower, Amelia Wood, Arthur Kay, Belinda and Emma Ralph, Camillo Toston, Catherine Stuart Grumbar, Connie McKimm, Dawn Wyatt, George Regan, Georgie Hilton, Grace McCloud, Hen Regan, James Frome,

Karen Randall, Lucy Mee, Ludovica Pilot, Louisa Boscawen, Michael Makonnen, Milla Lupton, Shivani Amin, Tish Frome and Veronica Goulder.

Thanks again to Alpesh Chauhan for meticulously testing every single recipe in this recipe book and helping me to become a better cook.

Thank you to Auntie Dolly for being such a source of inspiration to me – I hope when I'm your age, I will be as charismatic, sharp-witted and independent as you are. Thank you to James for your love, support, patience, wisdom and ice baths. Thank you to Michael Regan for being so incredibly calm, generous and supportive, and for providing me with my VW van without which I could not have started SpiceBox. Thank you to Henrietta Regan for introducing me to cooking and India, for watching endless cookery shows with me during the early Noughties and for all your hard work with SpiceBox over the years (I'll pay you back one day!).

INDEX

Ebury Press, an imprint of Ebury Publishing,
20 Vauxhall Bridge Road,
London, SW1V 2SA

Ebury Press is part of the Penguin Random House group of companies
whose addresses can be found at **global.penguinrandomhouse.com**

Penguin
Random House
UK

First published by Ebury Press in 2021
www.penguin.co.uk

A CIP catalogue record for this book is available from the British Library

Publishing Director: Lizzy Gray
Editor: Celia Palazzo
Project Editor: Vicky Orchard
Design: Clare Skeats
Photography: Joff Lee and James Lee
Food styling: Rosie Ramsden
Food styling assistant: Rosie French
Prop styling: Tabitha Hawkins
Production: Lucy Harrison and Serena Nazareth

ISBN: 9781529106923

Colour origination by Altaimage Ltd, London
Printed and bound in Turkey by Elma Basim

The authorised representative in the EEA is Penguin Random House Ireland,
Morrison Chambers, 32 Nassau Street, Dublin D02 YH68.

Penguin Random House is committed to a sustainable future for
our business, our readers and our planet. This book is made from
Forest Stewardship Council® certified paper.